Sharing the Wealth

Sharing the Wealth

*Member Contributions and the
Exchange Theory of Party Influence
in the U.S. House of Representatives*

Damon M. Cann

State University of New York Press

Published by State University of New York Press, Albany

For information, contact State University of New York Press, Albany, NY
www.sunypress.edu

Production by Ryan Morris
Marketing by Michael Campochiaro

Library of Congress Cataloging-in-Publication Data

Cann, Damon M., 1976–
    Sharing the wealth : member contributions and the exchange theory of party influence in the
U.S. House of Representatives / Damon M. Cann.
        p. cm.
    Includes bibliographical references and index.
    ISBN 978-0-7914-7493-8 (hardcover : alk. paper)
    ISBN 978-0-7914-7494-5 (pbk. : alk. paper)   1.Campaign funds—United States.
2. United States. Congress. House.   3. Legislators—United States.   4. Political parties—
United States.   5. Power (Social sciences)—United States.   6. United States—Politics and
government.   I. Title.

JK1021.C36   2008
328.73'074—dc22

                                                                                        2007048684

10 9 8 7 6 5 4 3 2 1

For Clair, Cambria, and Ian

Contents

Illustrations

Figures

Tables

Preface

Ever since my college days, I have been captivated by the subject of campaign finance. Given that the bulk of academic studies provide scant evidence at best for a general relationship between campaign contributions and votes, I began to wonder where one might look to find specific effects. After all, as recent events surrounding Tom DeLay, Duke Cunningham, William Jefferson, and others suggest, money does seem to influence some members of Congress some of the time. It seemed to me that the goal for scholars should be to find the conditions under which campaign finance matters might influence politicians rather than continuing a fruitless search for general effects.

While studying the Republican takeover of Congress in the 1994 elections, I was intrigued by Newt Gingrich's strategy for improving the success of Republicans in U.S. House elections. For years, Gingrich had worked to develop a cadre of well-qualified congressional candidates by supporting Republican candidates for state legislatures. Monetary support came in part through GOPAC, a Gingrich-sponsored leadership political action committee (leadership PAC), distinct from the campaign committee supporting Gingrich's reelection. In 1994, Gingrich's GOPAC supported a number of candidates for office, some who he had helped as state legislators, and others who were incumbent members of Congress. I was also struck by the allegiance of members of the House Republican Conference to their new leader. I wondered if there might be a connection between Gingrich's efforts to support the election of Republican candidates and the increased level of party discipline in the 104th Congress, and resolved to gain a better understanding of these leadership PACs.

I was amazed to learn that members of Congress have been making contributions to other members of Congress for years. Although the first leadership PAC was formed in 1978, politicians had been an important source of campaign funds for their parties and for their fellow-party members even before the Federal Election Campaign Act (FECA) gave us the ability to comprehensively track such contributions. The general idea seemed to be that members of

Congress made contributions to other members of Congress (and also to their political party) to help the party obtain its collective goals. In return, party leaders mobilized their resources to further the personal political ambitions of its members. I embarked on this study of member contributions to examine some of the potential ways in which politicians and parties make exchanges to advance their respective goals, particularly focusing on exchanges involving member contributions to other members and to their parties. I am certainly not the first scholar to examine the development of member contributions. A great deal of excellent work has been done by Eric S. Heberlig, Marc Hetherington, Kris Kanthak, Robin Kolodny, Bruce Larson, Michael Malbin, Clyde Wilcox, and others. I hope the high esteem in which I hold their work is evidenced here.

Rather than trying to comprehensively cover all possible effects of member-to-member and member-to-party contributions,[1] I have two goals in this book. First, I seek to establish a framework that explains why these contributions can have powerful effects on the organization and operation of Congress. This will focus on exchanges among members of Congress (including party leaders) that advance the goals of both individual members and their parties. I contend that member contributions constitute an important part of the currency in these exchanges. Specifically, I contend that these exchanges have become an important source of power for American political parties. As such, I seek to clearly establish the relationship of this exchange framework to existing theories of partisan influence in Congress.

Second, I wish to offer several empirical examples of the types of influences that these contributions may have. Certainly there are more effects than those that I specifically explore here. I will, of course, strive to discuss other possible effects, highlighting the empirical evidence supporting these additional consequences of member-to-member and member-to-party contributions. It is my hope that readers will not only find the evidence herein to be persuasive, but also that readers will work to continue documenting the influences of these contributions.

While it is not the primary mission of this book to make prescriptions regarding campaign finance law, given that the research here finds that member-to-member and member-to-party contributions have demonstrable implications, it is impossible to proceed without at least a passing discussion of the normative implications of these contributions. Several of the scholars just mentioned have discussed some of the normative issues arising from member contributions; their work and some of my own ideas are discussed toward the end of the book; readers will be able to form their own conclusions.

At this point, I must also thank a number of scholars who made helpful comments on various portions of this book: John H. Aldrich, Scott Basinger, Jamie L. Carson, Stanley Feldman, Jay Goodliffe, Eric S. Heberlig, Brad Jones, Kris Kanthak, Bruce Larson, Helmut Norpoth, David W. Rohde, and Jeff Yates. Josh Putnam provided valuable research assistance. Any errors are, of course, my own.

CHAPTER 1

Introduction

Over the last twenty-five years, a remarkable phenomenon has developed in the U.S. Congress. While individuals, interest groups, corporations, labor unions, and parties all contribute money to support congressional candidates, members of Congress are themselves increasingly active as *contributors* to candidates and to political parties. Members make these contributions from funds they have raised for their own reelection campaigns or from a political action committee (PAC) formed for the express purpose of raising and redistributing funds. Indeed, some of the ethics questions surrounding former Republican House Majority Leader Tom DeLay center on contributions from his Texas-based leadership PAC that were allegedly illegally channeled into the campaigns of several Texas candidates through the Texas Republican Party.

While many scholars have noted the rise of members as contributors (Baker 1989, Wilcox 1989, Wilcox and Genest 1991, Kolodny 1998, Bedlington and Malbin 2003, Heberlig and Larson 2005), much of their work focuses on describing the increase in the amount of contributions that members of Congress donate to their parties and to each other. While the increase in the amount of funds available through these channels may seem novel, it is ultimately unimportant unless the use of such funding has observable consequences. While the rise of members as contributors is well-documented, the political impact of these donations is not thoroughly explored. Could member contributions affect the way in which Congress works? Consider the following two illustrations:

Tom Latham (R) has represented Iowa's 4th District in the U.S. House since 1994. The 4th District is evenly divided between Republicans and Democrats, and is considered one of Iowa's most competitive districts. Furthermore, redistricting in the 2002 elections changed 50% of the district, making it ripe for a Democratic challenge. Because Latham's seat was targeted by Republican leaders so as to retain control of the House in 2004, PACs sponsored by incumbent Republicans donated about $200,000 to Latham's campaign. This activism on the part of party members had one obvious effect—Latham carried the district 54–46. However, a less obvious effect is in Latham's voting. Indeed,

1

during the first session of the 109th Congress (2005), Latham voted with then House Majority Leader, Tom DeLay, on about 97% of all roll-call votes.

In addition to impacting members' voting behavior, member contributions might also affect congressional organization. Consider the appointment of committee chairs. At the outset of the 107th Congress, Jim Leach (R-IA) was forced to give up the chair of the House Banking and Financial Services Committee because of the six-year term limits Republicans placed on committee chairs in 1995. Marge Roukema, a moderate Republican from New Jersey, ranked second in seniority, having served on the committee for all of the twenty years she had spent in the House. By traditional standards, the gavel of the Banking Committee should have been hers.

However, the chairperson term limit was not the only committee reform made in the 104th Congress. The Republicans made it clear that seniority would be only one factor among others when choosing committee chairs. Roukema's party unity score (based on the standard *Congressional Quarterly* [*CQ*] score) in the 106th Congress was 78.5%, while her more junior opponents, Michael Oxley and Richard Baker, had scores of 92.5 and 92%, respectively. As an example of how money can demonstrate party loyalty, Oxley contributed $170,700 to Republican Party committees and $290,600 to Republican candidates in the 2000 election cycle; Baker had given $152,000 to party committees and $40,000 to fellow party candidates, while Roukema had made only $40,000 in contributions to Republican Party committees. Republican leaders must have been impressed with Oxley—they transferred part of the jurisdiction of the Energy and Commerce Committee (where Oxley had been serving) to the Banking and Financial Services to justify appointing Oxley as its chair even though he never held a position on that committee in the 106th Congress!

This book contends that exchanges involving member contributions are changing the political landscape in two important ways. First, member contributions have a *behavioral* effect on legislators. Leaders in Congress make contributions to rank-and-file members to win their loyalty in roll-call voting. To what extent do legislators actually reciprocate by supporting party leaders? Second, member contributions have an *institutional* effect on Congress. Candidates for congressional leadership positions, from the Speaker down to committee and subcommittee chairs, make contributions to their party and to other party members to build support for their leadership bids. To what extent have these contributions become part of the criteria used for selecting congressional leaders?

Perhaps more important than either the behavioral or institutional effect alone, these examples together suggest that political party leaders have found clever ways to harness the power of member-to-member and member-to-party contributions by entering exchanges with party members that further the goals of the party. Latham's example suggests that leaders may be able to use these contributions to promote unity in voting. Oxley's selection as chair of the

Banking and Financial Services Committee suggests that party leaders may distribute leadership positions in a way that rewards party unity and encourages members to raise money for the party and party candidates, a necessity in today's age where each election brings a stiff battle for majority control of Congress. Naturally, though, before drawing generalizable conclusions about the effects of member contributions, more systematic evidence is required than can be given in these simple examples.

Chapter 2 describes the legal framework within which member-to-member and member-to-party contributions are made and acquaints readers with existing descriptions of the members-as-contributors phenomena. Chapter 2 also presents recent data on member-to-member and member-to-party contributions and an analysis of which members of Congress are most likely to give and receive member-to-member contributions. This chapter also engages in a discussion of the proliferation of leadership PACs and member contributions over time.

Chapter 3 develops the theoretical framework for the remainder of the study, explaining why members of Congress donate to their respective parties and why legislators and the entire legislature may be affected by these contributions. By uniting disparate literatures on campaign finance, elections, and Congress, the chapter builds an exchange theory of member-to-member and member-to-party contributions. I explain how a feature of the electoral process (member contributions) may have important ramifications for the behavior of members of Congress and for the overall operation of Congress as an institution. Individuals seeking to gain or maintain a seat in Congress will be willing to offer their voting loyalty to congressional leaders who assist with the provision of the funds necessary to run a campaign. Further, members of Congress seeking to increase their power within Congress will exchange contributions in order to gain and maintain the leadership or committee chair positions they seek.

With the theoretical framework established, the remainder of the book focuses on documenting some of the consequences of member contributions. Chapter 4 is an empirical study of the relationship between leadership contributions and membership voting behavior. Previous work has suggested that no relationship exists between party committee contributions and members' voting loyalty (Damore and Hansford 1999, Cantor and Herrnson 1997). However, these studies do not consider the effect of contributions directly from party leaders. This is a significant omission given the different incentives faced by party committees and by party leaders. While party committees simply work to maximize the seats held by members of Congress, party leaders are engaged in the day-to-day struggle for the 218 votes needed to pass a bill in the House of Representatives. Results show that party leaders effectively exchange campaign contributions for increases in voting loyalty among the party's rank-and-file members.

Chapter 5 examines contests for committee chairs. While seniority has traditionally dominated the committee chair selection process, in recent years, political parties have violated the seniority rule with increasing frequency. Given the power that is centered in committee chairs, parties have a vested interest in making sure that ideologically loyal partisans occupy committee chair positions. I contend that political parties have taken control of the committee chair appointment process and have abandoned the seniority system in favor of an exchange-based system where the party grants committee chair positions as a reward for party loyalists and for prolific fund-raisers. I demonstrate this using both basic qualitative and sophisticated quantitative techniques.

Chapter 6 focuses on the House Appropriations Committee. Given the substantial amount of power vested in this committee, party leaders have often struggled to control this committee as a means of controlling what may be Congress' greatest power—the power of the purse. Nevertheless, historical attempts to reform the Appropriations Committee have not been smashing successes. Building on Aldrich and Rohde's (2000) work on post-1994 attempts to bring the Appropriations Committee under the control of the majority party, I show that Republican leaders have made inroads on the nonpartisan culture of the Appropriations Committee by exercising control over appointments to subcommittee chair positions on that committee. Further, the chapter shows that party leaders use subcommittee chair positions on Appropriations as an incentive to encourage fundraising on behalf of the party and party candidates.

Chapter 7 takes a qualitative approach to studying the role of member contributions in party leadership selection. While the role of member contributions in appointments to positions in the lower ranks of party leadership has been well-studied (Heberlig, Hetherington, and Larson 2006; Heberlig and Larson 2007), this chapter focuses on selecting the core leadership of the two major political parties (Speaker, majority/minority leader, majority/minority whip, and conference/caucus chairs). I show how fund-raising has become a key consideration in party leadership selection. Looking qualitatively at leadership contests through the late 1990s and early 2000s, I find that the leadership candidates who demonstrate the greatest capacity as fund-raisers tend to win the position they seek.

The book concludes with chapter 8 with a discussion of the overall impact of member-to-member and member-to-party contributions, with a particular focus on the implications of the exchange theory for the strength of congressional parties. It also encourages the reader to begin considering the normative implications of member contributions. These contributions allow members of Congress to receive twice as much money from interest groups by soliciting donations to their personal campaign fund as well as to their leadership PACs. Further, contributors who donate in support of a particular candidate may find that their contributions have simply been rerouted to another candidate who they did not want to support. This chapter discusses several possible legal reforms and their consequences. Finally, I argue that the importance of member contributions will only increase over time. With the disappearance of soft money in the wake of the Bipartisan Campaign Reform Act of 2002, parties are scrambling for new ways to raise more money. For cash-strapped parties, incumbent members of Congress have proven to be an excellent source for additional funds. This being the case, it seems that the importance of member-to-member and member-to-party contributions will only continue to increase with the passage of time.

CHAPTER 2

Candidates as Contributors?

Politicians with power have always helped to elect other like-minded politicians. Presidents, presidential candidates, and popular political figures regularly appear at fund-raisers or offer endorsements. However, over the last twenty-five years, politicians themselves have begun to contribute increasingly larger sums to candidates. Members of Congress making contributions to other candidates and to their parties is certainly not a new phenomenon. Large-scale, systematic analyses of these contributions prior to the 1970s are difficult, though, because it is only with the passage of the Federal Election Campaign Act that a comprehensive, centralized system for reporting and publishing campaign finance information was created. Kolodny (1998) offers a fascinating history of congressional campaign committees, piecing together available data to show that members of Congress have been an important source of political contributions (especially to the parties) for well over 100 years.

Kolodny shows that as early as the 1860s, party organizations placed "assessments" on members of the House and Senate (and even on their staff and members of the capitol police), averaging about $50, to support party activities. With this historical perspective, the "dues" levied by Republicans and Democrats on members of Congress today do not seem to be at all unusual (except perhaps for their size being greater than $25,000; see Herrnson 2004). Naturally, the more prominent the member of Congress, the more responsibility they have historically had for raising funds for the party and for party candidates. This is particularly true of party leaders. In the mid-twentieth century, Lyndon Johnson used the Democratic Congressional Campaign Committee to channel money from Texas oil millionaires to Democratic candidates, which arguably fueled his own rise to power. Interestingly, it appears to have been Johnson who "shook down" the oil millionaires rather than vice versa (Caro 1983, 602–62).

Our ability to accurately gauge comprehensive campaign contribution behavior begins with the passage of the Federal Election Campaign Act in 1971. Sundry amendments and court challenges (most notably *Buckley v. Valeo* [1976]) gradually modified the original law until the structure of the system was firmly established in the late 1970s. While the scope of the legal structure is quite broad, two unique features of the system are particularly important for the present discussion of members as contributors. First, the Supreme Court ruled in *Buckley* that campaign spending constitutes a form of political speech. Therefore, limits on the amount of money a candidate can spend are not constitutional as they inhibit candidates' right to free speech. While the *Buckley* ruling prohibited involuntary spending limits, the Court held that contribution limits can be established to preserve the integrity of the system. The result is a system where candidates can spend unlimited amounts of money, but they must raise it in relatively small increments. The much-heralded Bipartisan Campaign Reform Act of 2002 recently increased some of these contribution limits and indexed them to inflation, essentially guaranteeing that the limits will now increase over time.

The second important enduring feature of the system is the requirement that corporations, unions, and interest groups make contributions through political action committees. While individuals are permitted to make contributions, organizations are required to form separate PACs to administer their political contribution activities. Both individual contributors and PACs are required to disclose their contributions to federal candidates.

Given these constraints, the basic campaign finance process is simple— Candidates form a principal campaign committee (PCC) to manage the financial affairs of their campaign. Then, candidates receive contributions (subject to limits) through their PCC from one of four sources: (1) individual contributions, (2) party contributions, (3) self-funding, and (4) contributions from political action committees. While individual contributions often make up the largest percentage of a candidate's campaign funds (for incumbents, challengers, or open-seat candidates), incumbents are far more successful in raising PAC money than challengers. As a result, challengers must either raise more from individuals and parties or pick up the tab for their own campaign (Jacobson 2004).

Because incumbents are so successful at raising funds from PACs, a plethora of political scientists have wondered whether members of Congress exchange their votes quid pro quo with political donors. Corporate, labor, and interest group PACs have attracted enormous amounts of attention from scholars (Magleby and Nelson 1990, Wawro 2001, Grenzke 1989, Wright 1996, Herrnson 2004, and Jacobson 2004 to name just a few). The general result of these studies is that there is no evidence of general quid pro quo exchanges between members of Congress and PACs. It appears that PACs give to members who are already disposed to support the PAC's position rather than trying to "persuade" incumbents with a campaign contribution. It is worth noting, though, that Hall and Wayman (1990) find that members of Congress may spend more time and effort on issues of interest to their campaign contributors.

While businesses, labor unions, and interest groups are the most common sponsors of PACs (and have been the subject of many scholarly studies), there are no legal restrictions prohibiting individuals from forming PACs that are not associated with an organization. In fact, sitting members of Congress can, and often do, form PACs. In 1978 a sitting member of the House of Representatives, Henry Waxman (D-CA), became the first member of Congress to sponsor such a PAC. Waxman wanted to chair the Subcommittee on Health (a subcommittee of the Energy and Commerce Committee), but due to his lack of seniority, according to Democratic Party norms, he was unable to fill that position. However, Waxman speculated that he might be able to use his fund-raising skills to help him win the position. Waxman formed a PAC, raised funds, and redistributed the money (in increments of several thousand dollars) to other Democrats. His tactics proved to be persuasive—he ultimately won the subcommittee chair position he sought.

Because these politician-sponsored PACs are frequently formed by congressional leaders or by individuals who seek leadership positions, member-sponsored PACs are commonly referred to as "leadership PACs." Since 1978, more and more members of Congress have formed PACs. Figure 2.1 shows the number of active leadership PACs sponsored by members of the House of Representatives from 1978 to 2006. The general trend is clearly increasing, with substantial gains in the most recent election years. Naturally, with the proliferation of these PACs we have also witnessed a dramatic increase in the amount of money raised and redistributed through these member-led PACs to a point where sitting members of Congress are now a major source of campaign funds. While the Bipartisan Campaign Reform Act of 2002 (BCRA) made significant changes in the campaign finance system, it placed no regulations on leadership PACs. In fact, Senator John McCain (R-AZ), one of the sponsors of the BCRA, maintains a leadership PAC of his own.

FIGURE 2.1 Number of Leadership PACs Sponsored by Members of the House of Representatives, 1978–2006

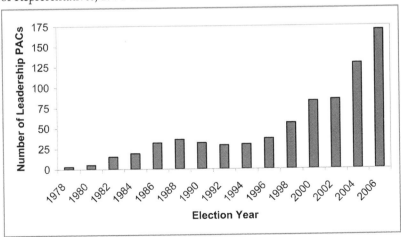

SOURCE: Buchler (2002), The Almanac of Federal PACs 1997–98, and the Center for Responsive Politics http://www.opensecrets.org.

In addition to leadership PACs, members of Congress make contributions directly from their own reelection funds. Many candidates, particularly safe incumbents, raise far more money than they spend. Some candidates save their excess funds in a "war chest," either to act as a deterrent to future challengers (Box-Steffensmeier 1996) or more likely as insurance in the event that a legislator faces a stiff challenge in the future (Goodliffe 2001). Notwithstanding the political importance of these uses for war chests, many members of Congress share at least a portion of their excess reelection funds with other members of Congress. In this way, candidate-contributors can give the maximum contribution twice—once from a leadership PAC, and again from their personal campaign funds.

Growth of Member Contributions

The FECA reforms requiring the formation of political action committees opened the possibility of individual members of Congress forming leadership PACs. Since the formation of the first leadership PAC in 1978, the volume of funds contributed from members of Congress to other members has increased substantially. Figure 2.2 illustrates the level of contributions from House and Senate candidates to other House and Senate candidates in 1978 through 2004. Two features are worth particular note: First, there is a general trend of increases in member contributions over time, and second, the level of member contributions appears to have exploded after the Republican takeover of Congress.[1]

FIGURE 2.2 House and Senate Member-to-Member Contributions, 1978–2004

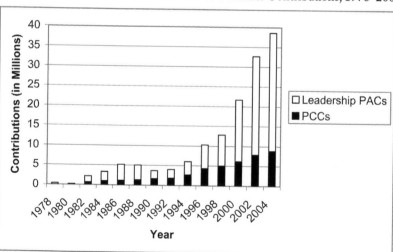

SOURCE: Buchler (2002), Belington and Malbin (2003), and Center for Responsive Politics http://www.opensecrets.org.

The prevailing explanation for the effusive growth in member contributions is the increased competition for majority control of Congress. Heberlig and Larson (2005), for instance, show that as the seat margin between Republicans and Democrats narrows, the amount of member contributions increases. Kolodny (1998), Kuhn (1999), and Currinder (2003) make similar arguments regarding the pursuit of majority status as a driving factor behind member contributions.

The Allocation of Member Contributions

Given the dramatic growth in member-to-member and member-to-party contributions, it is natural to wonder which members of Congress are making these contributions and whether some candidates are more likely to receive contributions from incumbents. A number of studies show that PACs consider a number of factors (including incumbency, party, and electoral competitiveness) when making decisions regarding to whom they will contribute (Magleby and Nelson 1990, Sorauf 1992, Herrnson 2004). We now turn to a discussion of who receives and who gives these contributions in the specific context of leadership PACs in U.S. House elections in the 1999–2000, 2001–2002, and 2003–2004 election cycles.[2]

Who Receives These Contributions?

The campaign finance literature shows that PACs in general are strategic in the allocation of their resources, with PACs targeting much of their money on the basis of incumbency, party identification, competitiveness, and ideology (Grier and Munger 1991, 1993; Gopoian 1984). While Kanthak (2007) makes a notable contribution to understanding the potential influence of ideology on contributions from leadership PACs, the literature on member contributions is less well-developed in regards to the effects of incumbency and competitiveness.

INCUMBENCY

Members of Congress who make contributions may do so simply to try to win favor with their fellow-incumbents. If this is the case, incumbents would be simply passing money around to one another, potentially with little effect on the composition of the legislature and on electoral outcomes. However, members of Congress may try to target their contributions to challengers and to open-seat candidates to help build their party's majority. Table 2.1 shows the percentage of all contributions from leadership PACs and from PCCs that went to incumbents, challengers, and open-seat candidates in the 1999–2004 period. Incumbents took about three-fourths of all member-to-member contributions while open-seat candidates and challengers took up just over 10 percent each. It is remarkable that even though there are far more challengers (counting both primary and general election challengers) than incumbents and open-seat candidates put together, they receive only slightly more than one-tenth of all member-to-member contributions.

Sharing the Wealth

TABLE 2.1 Percentage of Member-to-Member Funds by Incumbency Status

	Incumbents	Open Seat	Challengers
Percentage of All Leadership Contributions	75.2%	13.1%	11.7%
Number of Candidates in Each Category	1,195	862	2,205

NOTE: Includes only major party candidates.

SOURCE: Data for all of the tables in this chapter are from the Federal Elections Commission (FEC), Center for Responsive Politics, and Michael Malbin.

A second matter of interest is how the funds are distributed within each category of incumbency status. We need to know whether a few candidates in each category are getting relatively large contributions, or if many candidates in each category receive relatively small contributions. Table 2.2 shows the percentage of candidates in each incumbency category who receive contributions from other members. Nearly 90 percent of incumbents receive at least some contribution from a leadership PAC or from another candidate's PCC. Those who lost their primary election received greater support (likely because their colleagues tried to pull them through a tough primary), receiving an average of nearly $60,000 from leadership PACs and PCCs. Incumbents who won their primary election averaged about $27,000 in contributions from other candidates. In contrast to incumbents, challengers and open-seat candidates receive very little support in primary elections. However, about one-fifth of challengers and over one-third of open-seat candidates who advance to the general election receive contributions. In short, the bulk of these funds tend to go to incumbents, but some challengers and open-seat candidates who win primary elections receive assistance from other candidates. It is natural to wonder, then, what determines which candidates receive contributions and how much they get. One natural explanation from the campaign finance literature is that competitive candidates tend to raise more money (Magleby and Nelson 1990, Wright 1996).

COMPETITIVENESS AND MEMBER CONTRIBUTIONS

Table 2.2 already shows that challengers and open-seat candidates who are successful in winning a primary election get more support from member-contributors. Table 2.3 further illustrates that competitive candidates[3] receive more support from member-donors.[4] Examining all general election candidates, Table 2.3 shows that competitive candidates raise far more member donations

TABLE 2.2 Percentage of Major-Party Candidates Receiving Member Contributions and Average Size of Contribution by Incumbency Status

	Incumbents		Open Seat		Challenger		All	
	Won Primary	Lost Primary	Won Primary	Lost Primary	Won Primary	Lost Primary	Won Primary	Lost Primary
Percent Receiving Member Contributions	87.2%	88.9%	36.7%	6.3%	20.0%	2.4%	54.9%	4.6%
Mean Amount of Contributions (Std. Dev.)	$26,582 (57,681)	$59,229 (91,598)	$23,172 (48,155)	$543 (6,737)	$4,978 (21,934)	$180 (3,641)	$17,454 (46,658)	$864 (11,497)

TABLE 2.3 Percentage of Major–Party Candidates Receiving Member Contributions by Incumbency Status and Electoral Competitiveness

	Incumbents		Open Seat		Challenger		All	
	Comp.	Non-Comp.	Comp.	Non-Comp.	Comp.	Non-Comp.	Comp.	Non-Comp.
Percent Receiving Member Contributions	95.9%	84.7%	41.1%	29.5%	44.1%	14.4%	68.2%	49.9%
Mean Contribution (Std. Dev.)	$83,218 (93,068)	$10,390 (26,226)	$31,534 (51,069)	$11,641 (39,401)	$21,484 (40,628)	$1,561 (13,176)	$53,194 (77,697)	$6,448 (17,270)

than noncompetitive candidates. Almost 70 percent of competitive candidates receive contributions from other candidates. This pattern of targeting contributions to competitive candidates holds for challengers, open-seat candidates, and incumbents, though competitive incumbents are the most likely to receive a contribution. While a high percentage of non-competitive incumbents receive contributions from other members, they receive an average contribution of a mere $10,000, while competitive incumbents raise an average of over $80,000.

PARTY DIFFERENCES IN MEMBER CONTRIBUTIONS

Clearly, the parties are not identical in their allocation strategies. Republicans are more prolific in raising member-to-member contributions. In the 1999–2004 period, about 63 percent of member contributions went to Republican candidates, leaving just 37 percent for Democratic candidates. In addition to differences in the amount of money raised and redistributed by members of the two parties, the parties may also differ in their strategies for allocating these resources. Certainly in the case of resources controlled directly by the party (contributions from party committees) this is the case. Jacobson (1985-86) shows that in the 1982 elections, Republicans did a much better job of targeting party resources to competitive races than Democrats. This resulted in a midterm seat loss in Congress that was much smaller than forecasting models predicted. Given that parties may differ in their allocation strategies for funds controlled directly by the party, it may also be that one party is better than the other at getting members to target their contributions to candidates who both need the money and who will benefit most from receiving additional financial support.

Additionally, depending on majority status, parties may try to target their resources differently. Currinder (2003) hypothesizes that member contributors in the majority party should pursue a maintaining strategy—that is, they should donate money to endangered incumbents in order to preserve their majority. In contrast, the minority party should follow an expansive strategy whereby they donate heavily to open-seat candidates and challengers in an attempt to take the majority. If one party is better at allocating their resources than the other, we would expect to see one party donating more funds to competitive candidates (overall) than the other party. If majority status affects the way in which members make contributions, we should expect Republicans to donate most heavily to incumbents (and perhaps to open-seat candidates), while Democrats will donate most heavily to non-incumbents. Table 2.4 shows the results for Democrats and Table 2.5 shows the results for Republicans. Both tables include only candidates involved in a general election.

In contrast to Currinder's (2003) expectations, both Republican and Democratic member-to-member contributions follow a similar pattern. Both parties focus their contributions on competitive elections, with 78.2%

TABLE 2.4 Percentage of Democratic Candidates Receiving Member Contributions by Incumbency Status and Electoral Competitiveness

| | Incumbents | | Open Seat | | Challenger | | All | |
	Comp.	Non-Comp.	Comp.	Non-Comp.	Comp.	Non-Comp.	Comp.	Non-Comp.
Percent Receiving Leader Contributions	94.0%	77.5%	24.6%	16.0%	29.7%	13.3%	57.0%	45.2%
Mean Contribution (Std. Dev.)	$72,443 (76,165)	$7,714 (18,718)	$23,983 (47,979)	$5,189 (17,797)	$16,472 (38,786)	$2,017 (17,784)	$42,799 (65,230)	$5,002 (18,443)

TABLE 2.5 Percentage of Republican Candidates Receiving Member Contributions by Incumbency Status and Electoral Competitiveness

	Incumbents		Open Seat		Challenger		All	
	Comp.	Non-Comp.	Comp.	Non-Comp.	Comp.	Non-Comp.	Comp.	Non-Comp.
Percent Receiving Leader Contributions	97.4%	92.2%	55.2%	44.4%	60.8%	15.5%	78.2%	54.9%
Mean Contribution (Std. Dev.)	$91,512 (103,718)	$13,150 (31,974)	$37,957 (53,068)	$18,810 (53,517)	$27,257 (42,161)	$1,095 (5,271)	$62,437 (86,365)	$7,936 (26,411)

of competitive Republican candidates receiving contributions from other Republican candidates (as opposed to just 54.9% of non-competitive candidates, many of whom are incumbents) and 57% of Democrats receiving contributions from Democratic candidates (vs. 45.2% of non-competitive Democrats). It appears that both parties follow the same strategy of providing particularly strong support to their endangered incumbents, making small token contributions to safe incumbents, and supporting competitive challengers and open-seat candidates to try to build their ranks. There is no support for the notion that the majority party pursues a maintaining strategy while the minority party pursues an expansive strategy.

Notwithstanding the general similarities in the donation patterns of members of both parties, two major differences between the parties stand out in Tables 2.4 and 2.5. First, across all categories, Republicans support a higher percentage of their candidates than Democrats. Second, with the exception of non-competitive challengers (the least valuable contribution type), Republicans have a higher average contribution across all categories. This is almost certainly a result of the Republicans raising and redistributing more money than the Democrats in this time period.

Who Makes These Contributions?

More and more members are forming leadership PACs. In the 2004 election cycle, 129 members of the House sponsored a leadership PAC. In addition to those members, many more drew money from their PCC to give to their party or to other candidates. We now turn to a discussion of which members of Congress make contributions and how much they give. The figures focus on contributions from members' PCCs and from leadership PACs to party committees or to other candidates in the 1999–2000, 2001–2002, and 2003–2004 election cycles.

INCUMBENCY

Among the host of advantages associated with incumbency is fund-raising (Jacobson 2004). Given that many incumbents don't need all of the money they raise, one would expect incumbents to be more likely to make contributions to other members of Congress. In contrast, challengers and open-seat candidates are already hard-pressed for funds and are unlikely to share funds with other candidates when they themselves have less money than they need.

Table 2.6 shows the average amount of money given to party committees and to other candidates from major party candidates in the 2000 general election. Incumbents give over 98% of all member-to-member and member-to-party contributions, with just a few open-seat candidates and challengers making smaller contributions. This is not surprising, given that challengers and open-seat candidates face greater difficulties in raising funds and winning races, and they must use virtually all of the money they are able to raise.

TABLE 2.6 Who Gives Member-to-Member Contributions by Incumbency Status

	Incumbents	Open Seat	Challengers
Mean Contribution	$131,925	$6,631	$1,195
(Std. Dev.)	(211,711)	(31,355)	(12,225)
n	1189	246	1017

NOTE: Based on major-party candidates in the 2000, 2002, and 2004 general elections.

ELECTORAL SAFETY

One reason why incumbents may be such prolific givers is that they generally face little competition in their reelection campaigns (Ferejohn 1977, Cover 1977). Safe incumbents are then free to redistribute their excess funds to help their party or fellow-party candidates. In contrast, incumbents facing strong challengers may need to use all of their resources simply to maintain their seat.

Table 2.7 shows the relationship between electoral safety and member contributions. Safe incumbents give nearly twice as much, on average, as incumbents who eventually won less than 60 percent of the vote. If the cutoff for determining a "competitive" race is dropped to 55 percent of the vote share, the average contribution drops to $61,000. In short, incumbents who are in danger of losing their seats use more of their resources to ensure their reelection while incumbents with safe seats are rather generous, averaging almost $150,000 in contributions to their party and to other candidates.

TABLE 2.7 Incumbent Member-to-Member Contributions by Electoral Safety

	Safe Seat	Competitive Seat
Mean Contribution	$145,940	$75,924
(Std. Dev.)	(219,843)	(164,337)
n	951	238

NOTE: Based on incumbent major-party candidates in the 2000, 2002, and 2004 general elections. Safe seats are defined as those where the incumbent won at least 60% of the vote; competitive seats are those where the incumbent won less than 60% of the vote.

TABLE 2.8 Member-to-Member Contributions from House Leaders, Committee Chairs, Committee Chair Candidates, and Other Incumbents

	Leader	Chair/Chair Candidate	Other Safe Incumbent	Other Competitive Incumbent
Mean Contribution	$960,348	$224,196	$117,378	$55,895
(Std. Dev.)	(479,326)	(310,993)	(148,440)	(95,816)
n	24	84	860	221

LEADERSHIP

Members of Congress with high-profile positions in the institution tend to attract more campaign contributions (Cox and Magar 1999). Thus, party leaders and committee chairs are more likely to find themselves flush with campaign funds but electorally safe. Further, these leaders may be interested in helping to gain or maintain majority status (Currinder 2003, Heberlig and Larson 2005) or to encourage the loyalty of party members. Additionally, these congressional leaders are responsible for helping the party raise funds to perpetuate its operations. Even members of Congress who don't yet hold such positions of power (but seek to hold them) may be interested in raising large amounts of money to demonstrate their ability as fund-raisers if they were selected for a leadership position.

Table 2.8 compares the average level of contributions from the top four leaders of each party, sitting and aspiring committee chairs, and all other incumbents. In the three election cycles in the 1999–2004 period, the top four leaders of each party made an average contribution of nearly $1 million each. Committee chairs and committee chair candidates averaged contributions of about $225,000. Other safe incumbents raised smaller but significant amounts, while non-leader, non-committee chair incumbents in competitive races (less than 60 percent of the vote) averaged only about $55,000 in contributions. In short, individuals with high-profile institutional positions and those who seek them contribute far more than even their safe incumbent counterparts.

MEMBER AMBITIONS

The importance of ambition as a factor encouraging member contributions was illustrated in Table 2.8 by evaluating the contribution behavior of committee chair candidates. The strategic elements of making contributions were discussed in detail by Wilcox (1989) and by Wilcox and Genest (1991), who were among the early observers of the member-contributor phenomenon. They emphasize that members generally form leadership PACs to further their political ambitions. Specifically, members who are seeking higher office (especially the presidency) or seeking a leadership position are more likely to sponsor a leadership PAC and to donate from their PCC. Similarly, Heberlig and Larson (2005) show that sitting leaders donate far more to other members and to the parties than non-leaders. Tables 2.9, 2.10, and 2.11 show the top ten member contributors in the 2000, 2002, and 2004 elections, respectively. The contribution figures in the tables are the sum of contributions made from leadership PACs and PCCs to other members and to party committees. The tables also show the position that each of the top ten donors in each year held in Congress before the election as well as the position they aspired to hold in the next Congress (or in the near future).[5] Where no ambition is listed, the member simply sought to maintain their current position.

TABLE 2.9 Top 10 Member Donors, 2000 U.S. House Elections

Member	Amount Given to Party Committees and Candidates	Position	Ambition
Dick Armey (R-TX)	$1,354,084	Majority Leader	Speaker
Dennis Hastert (R-IL)	$1,288,128	Speaker	
Tom DeLay (R-TX)	$1,270,491	Rep. Whip	Majority Leader
David Dreier (R-CA)	$1,257,549	Rules Committee Chair	Retain Chair in Spite of Term Limit
Nancy Pelosi (D-CA)	$1,133,009		Dem. Whip
Dick Gephardt (D-MO)	$1,125,381	Minority Leader	Speaker
Charles Rangel (D-NY)	$997,500	Ranking Dem., Ways and Means	Ways and Means Chair
Stenny Hoyer (D-MD)	$928,000		Dem. Whip
Christopher Cox (R-CA)	$873,000	Rep. Policy Committee Chair	
Jerry Lewis (R-CA)	$839,849	Defense Subcommittee on Appropriations Chair	Appropriations Committee Chair

TABLE 2.10 Top 10 Member Donors, 2002 U.S. House Elections

Member	Amount Given to Party Committees and Candidates	Position	Ambition
Nancy Pelosi (D-CA)	$1,314,250	Minority Whip	Minority Leader
Tom DeLay (R-TX)	$1,268,855	Majority Leader	Speaker
Dennis Hastert (R-IL)	$1,211,500	Speaker	
Charles Rangel (D-NY)	$1,187,000	Ranking Dem., Ways and Means	Ways and Means Chair
Bob Menendez (D-NJ)	$1,013,856	Dem. Caucus Vice-Chair	Dem. Caucus Chair
Stenny Hoyer (D-MD)	$966,725		Minority Whip
Bill Thomas (R-CA)	$887,500	Ways and Means Chair	Retain Chair in spite of Term Limits
Nita Lowey (D-NY)	$857,500	DCCC Chair	Majority Status
Roy Blunt (R-MO)	$812,344	Chief Majority Deputy Whip	Majority Whip
Michael Oxley (R-OH)	$782,625	Banking and Financial Services Chair	Retain Chair

The tables show that the most prolific member-donors were individuals holding significant offices, individuals seeking a leadership position, or committee chair candidates. Both parties are generally well-represented in the top ten, with the exception of 2004, where eight of the top ten member contributors were Republicans. The evidence in the table buttresses the results of Heberlig and Larson (2005) in showing that sitting leaders of both parties gave substantial sums of money to other candidates and to their parties. However, two notes are in order. First, with the possible exception of the Speaker, all sitting party leaders generally hope to move farther up the leadership ladder, making contributions important for them. Second, party leaders are not the only ones on these lists—the top ten in each year also consist of members who seek party or committee leadership positions. For example, neither Nancy Pelosi nor Stenny Hoyer held a position in the core leadership of the Democratic Party in the 106th Congress. Yet, both were hopeful that the Democrats would take control of Congress, which would have likely led to the promotions of Gephardt and Bonior to Speaker and majority leader, respectively, leaving the majority whip position open. Though Democrats failed to take control of the House in the 2000 elections, Bonior retired in 2001 and Pelosi and Hoyer ultimately faced off for the minority whip position he

TABLE 2.11　Top 10 Member Donors, 2004 U.S. House Elections

Member	Amount Given to Party Committees and Candidates	Position	Ambition
Jerry Lewis (R-CA)	$1,790,000		Appropriations Chair
Dennis Hastert (R-IL)	$1,754,971	Speaker	
Roy Blunt (R-MO)	$1,740,039	Majority Whip	Majority Leader
Stenny Hoyer (D-MD)	$1,460,000	Minority Whip	Majority Leader
Nancy Pelosi (D-CA)	$1,217,000	Minority Leader	Speaker
Hal Rogers (R-KY)	$1,090,000		Appropriations Chair
Eric Cantor (R-VA)	$1,041,792	Chief Majority Deputy Whip	Party Leadership
Ralph Regula (R-OH)	$1,037,000		Appropriations Chair
Tom Reynolds (R-NY)	$1,021,500	NRCC Chair	Maintain Majority Status
Tom DeLay (R-TX)	$1,006,278	Majority Leader	Speaker

vacated. As far as committee leadership goes, Charles Rangel, like Pelosi and Hoyer, thought that the Democrats might win control of Congress in the 2000 elections, and wanted to make sure that he was elevated from ranking member of the Ways and Means Committee to its chair if the Democrats indeed won. David Dreier was beginning a campaign just to keep his seat as chair of the Rules Committee—he knew he faced a term limit that would force him from his position at the end of the 108th Congress, and that other chairs had not been granted waivers. Dreier's persistent fund-raising efforts and diligent support of the Republican leadership won him a term-limit waiver and allowed him to keep his seat.

Implications

Given that member-to-member and member-to-party contributions are dramatically increasing, and given that members and party leaders seem to use them to further their ambitions, it seems worthwhile to embark on a detailed study of the consequences of member donations. To begin such an exploration, we must consider the relationships between member-donors and those who receive member contributions. This exploration will allow us to construct a theoretical framework that explains the consequences of member-to-member and member-to-party contributions. These tasks are pursued in chapter 3.

CHAPTER 3

The Exchange Theory of Party Influence

Having seen that many members of Congress make sizable contributions from their personal campaign funds and/or from a leadership PAC, it is natural to wonder why they would part with funds they raised for themselves. Given that they must devote substantial time and energy to raising these funds (Jacobson 2004), it seems reasonable that they would only do so under circumstances that would bring them greater benefit than keeping the money (or saving themselves the cost of raising it).

Some scholars have argued that members of Congress sometimes raise more money than necessary by "accident" because they expected a strong challenger but ultimately face a weak challenger instead (Ansolabehere and Snyder 2000; Goodliffe 2004, 2007).[1] It could be that members of Congress simply pass on these excess funds to the party or to other members of Congress. However, the notion of excess funds as accidents cannot explain the dramatic rise in member contributions in the last twenty years unless one assumes that candidates make many more "accidents" in estimating the amount of funds needed for election today than they did ten or twenty years ago. Rather than writing off the member contributions phenomenon as a non-systematic series of accidents, I contend that members of the House intentionally raise these funds and contribute to other candidates and to their parties in situations where doing so advances their personal ambitions.

Given that members of Congress seem to allocate these contributions in ways that help their party (focusing on helping same-party incumbents and competitive challengers and open-seat candidates), it is similarly impossible to consider explanations for member contributions without also considering the goals of political parties and how political parties can induce members of Congress to allocate their personal campaign resources in a way that benefits the party. In this chapter, I will explain how member contributions have become a common thread that runs through the major goals of both political parties and through the goals of individual members of Congress. More specifically, I will consider the relevance of money in achieving electoral success and power within Congress for individual legislators and explain the mechanisms linking the member contributions, the goals of members of Congress, and the goals of the political parties (and party leaders).

Given the broad spectrum of possible consequences of member-to-member and member-to-party contributions, this requires unifying literature from several diverse literatures in political science. We begin by discussing the campaign finance literature with an eye toward understanding the structure of the campaign finance system, descriptions of member contributions, and strategies behind making such contributions. We must also consider the literature on the U.S. Congress. This is essential because we must understand the goals of both individual legislators and the goals of political parties, particularly in light of dominant theories of political party influence (Rohde 1991; Aldrich and Rohde 1997–98; Cox and McCubbins 1993, 2005). Finally, because member contributions are a feature of the electoral process, we must consider the literature on elections and connect it to the institutional literature on Congress. In uniting these three literatures, we may establish a framework from which to assess how a feature tied to the electoral process (campaign contributions) ultimately affects the way in which members of Congress behave and how Congress as an institution operates. This will be done by emphasizing exchanges between members of Congress and their parties that ultimately further the goals of both entities.

Campaign Finance Perspective

Many campaign finance studies tend to focus on the question, "Who gave how much, and to whom?" Major works on campaign finance (e.g., Magleby and Nelson 1990, Sabato and Simpson 1996, Sorauf 1992) give comprehensive answers to these questions for contributions from individuals and PACs, but devote cursory attention at best, to member contributions. Nevertheless, several scholars have noted and documented the contribution activities of members of Congress. Wilcox (1989, 1990) and Wilcox and Genest (1991) identified early on that incumbent members, especially leaders, were sharing campaign funds with other members. They noted an increase through the 1980s in member-to-member donations. Further, they noted that the most frequent contributors were leaders, committee chairs, or individuals who wanted to become leaders or committee chairs. Additionally, they showed that members of Congress contemplating a run for the presidency frequently use leadership PAC money to finance the early portion of their campaign. More recently, Bedlington and Malbin (2003) extrapolate the trends in member-to-member giving and make note of the biggest donors and recipients. They also list the names of members who made the largest amounts of member-to-member and member-to-party contributions. Further, they document a dramatic increase in member-to-member giving beginning with elections to the 104th Congress.

While campaign finance scholars have helped to bring some notoriety to the leader-contributor phenomenon, in many instances they have stopped short of the ultimate goal. An expanding source of funding, however novel, is ultimately unimportant unless it can be shown that the funds have some real political impact. All of these authors have discussed possible reasons why members of Congress exert their effort to raise funds that they will simply redistribute to other members or to their party. The three possibilities that arise most frequently merit further discussion: First, the notion that funds are raised and redistributed in pursuit of majority status; second, the hypothesis that leadership aspirants make contributions to win favor with party members who will support their bids for party or committee leadership positions; and third, the question of whether congressional leaders are able to effectively "buy" votes from candidates who seek party support for their reelection effort.

A few scholars have actually moved beyond positing these effects to empirically evaluate the implications of member contributions. Such tests have most often focused on the role of member contributions in the pursuit of majority control of the House of Representatives. Currinder (2003) notes that if majority control is the major goal of parties raising and redistributing money, one would expect parties to follow different strategies when making contributions depending on whether or not they hold majority status. She shows that the majority party generally donates most heavily to incumbents in order to preserve their majority. In contrast, the minority party is more supportive of challengers and open-seat candidates as they must gain seats beyond those which they already hold if they are to win a majority. The idea that the member-contributor phenomenon has skyrocketed since 1994 is supported in other studies of member-to-member contributions (Heberlig and Larson 2005; Kuhn 1999; Heberlig, Hetherington, and Larson 2006). The battle for majority status certainly helps explain why member contributions have become more important today than ever before; however, the intense, costly battles for control of the House that surface biannually are not the only important consequence of the increase in the importance of these contributions. Moreover, just showing that the parties need the money does not explain why members make these donations. Party fund-raising from members is a classic collective action problem because an individual member's contribution to the party or to another candidate will have little effect on the party's chances of winning majority status. Nevertheless, larger aggregate contributions could swing majority status one way or the other. Since individual members receive the collective benefit (majority status) with or without their contribution, it is in members' individual interests to shirk their fund-raising duties unless the party provides a selective incentive (or uses coercion) to lead members to support the party (Olson 1965).

Fewer studies have investigated the other two propositions just mentioned. Still, for example, Cantor and Herrnson (1997) and Damore and Hansford (1999) have pursued promising efforts to link voting unity in the House of Representatives and campaign contributions from party sources. However, both only consider contributions from party committees (e.g., the National Republican Congressional Committee [NRCC] and the Democratic Congressional Campaign Committee [DCCC]). Work in this direction with leadership PAC and PCC contributions remains to be done. Heberlig (2003) shows that members of Congress who contribute to party causes are more likely to receive a seat on a prestigious committee. Further, Heberlig, Hetherington, and Larson (2006) show that making contributions to the party and to party candidates increases the chances of a member of Congress moving into the extended party leadership (e.g., low- to mid-level posts in the party whip systems). Greater consideration of the role of member contributions in these areas remains important in order to reinforce and expand the claims made in these studies.

Congressional Perspective

While campaign finance scholars have at least theorized that legislative loyalty may have electoral origins, and that campaign contributions could affect leadership selection and legislative organization, these ideas have not yet found root in the congressional literature. This is particularly surprising in light of the vigorous debate over the strength of parties that has absorbed the attention of many congressional scholars in recent years. Congressional scholars tend to approach the question of party loyalty from a more institutional basis.

Cox and McCubbins (1993, 1994, 2005) articulate the party cartel theory of party influence, contending that members of the majority party face severe collective action problems. In order to achieve party goals, members of Congress cede power to party leaders, most specifically in the realm of negative agenda control (the ability to defeat bills that the majority party dislikes). Cox and McCubbins argue that the power of negative agenda control is consistently applied by the majority party leadership even in periods where conventional wisdom holds that party strength in the House was weak (e.g., the 1960s). While one must certainly not underestimate the importance of negative agenda control, if we are to believe (as many do today) that parties have positive powers (advantages in passing bills that the majority party likes), we must consider theories of party influence that might explain how parties gain additional powers.

In their Conditional Party Government (CPG) hypothesis, Aldrich and Rohde (Rohde 1991, Aldrich 1995, Aldrich and Rohde 1997–98, Aldrich and Rohde 2000) argue that the costs of organizing to overcome collective action problems change over time. These costs will be lowest when parties are externally polarized and internally homogeneous. In the presence of these two conditions, party leaders will find that the benefits of organizing coalitions out-weigh the costs. Moreover, only in the presence of these conditions will members of Congress find it advantageous (and permissible to their constituency) to join a party coalition (see also, Aldrich and Rohde 1997–98, 2000, 2001).

This view, while sophisticated and logical, has at least one undesirable property. In the conditional party government perspective, the ability for a party to wield power is not a function of anything the party does—it is merely changes in the ideological composition of the chamber that brings party leaders power or takes it away. This perspective leaves little room for active party leadership—if a party is already homogeneous and distant from the other party, there would be less need for leaders to persuade members to vote in a specific way. In the CPG perspective, parties seem to lack the tools to actively cultivate voting unity. A complementary theory of party governance could specify mechanisms by which parties can actively pursue power.

Krehbiel (1993) echoes similar sentiments by challenging scholars to demonstrate that "significant party behavior" actually occurs. For Krehbiel, significant party behavior occurs when legislators vote with the party in spite of their constituency's wishes rather than voting with the party because of the constituency's wishes. His empirical searches for party effects (1991, 1993) find no evidence of significant party behavior. However, he admits (1993) that if we were searching in a house to find party loyalty, he has merely checked a few rooms.[2] Rather than calling off the search for significant party behavior after searching the attic, I contend that Krehbiel has simply looked in the wrong places for party effects. Certainly, the large sums of money flowing from party leaders and from leadership aspirants to candidates and the contributions from members of Congress to their parties are obvious places to search for party effects. I contend that member-to-member and member-to-party campaign contributions are a critical tool that parties can use to build party loyalty.

The Electoral Perspective

The shortcomings of the congressional and campaign finance approaches can be resolved by considering the ambitions of members and their parties in an electoral framework. Schlesinger (1966) contends that politicians' activities are driven by their ambitions. Fenno's (1973) famous trichotomy of ambitions has been broadly accepted as a statement of politicians' goals. Fenno contends that members of Congress seek election (or reelection), power in Washington, and good public policy. Of course, at times, these goals conflict with each other (Aldrich and Rohde 2000). A member of Congress may seek a party leadership position (power in Washington), but in order to win that position, they may need to make ideological compromises (which may conflict with their desire to make what they consider "good" public policy). Alternatively, members seeking a leadership position may at times be required to sacrifice some of their own campaign funds or may need to vote more frequently with their party, both of which may hamper their reelection goals (though members will be careful minimize the risk of losing reelection).

While all three member ambitions are certainly important factors in many facets of legislators' decision making, the primacy of the electoral ambition cannot be disputed, as election is a prerequisite for obtaining power in Washington and for crafting good public policy (Mayhew 1974). Nevertheless, there are many electorally safe members with deeply held desires to gain more power or to see certain policies enacted. Further, it has been shown that while winning is important, members do not behave strictly as vote-maximizers (see, e.g., Milyo 2001). Thus, it seems unwise to excessively discount the nonelective goals of legislators.

Not only do the electoral ambitions of individual legislators loom large, but the two major American political parties also have electoral ambitions. Success in this goal naturally requires politicians to be successful in their individual electoral goals but becomes more complicated when one considers how parties can best allocate their limited campaign resources to best achieve their electoral ambitions.

The Exchange Framework and the Mutual Advancement of Member and Party Goals

Sinclair (1983), Cox and McCubbins (1993, 2005), and Currinder (2003) have all suggested that political parties will best be able to advance their goals when party leaders structure the congressional world in such a way that support of the party also furthers the individual ambitions of party members. Indeed, Aldrich (1995) contends that members adopt a partisan identification specifically because it is in their best interest to do so. Historically, party leaders who exercise their powers such that it is beneficial for members to support the party are particularly effective (Cooper and Brady 1981).

In their party cartel theory, Cox and McCubbins (1993, 1994, 2005) contend that certain powers (particularly negative agenda control) are simply inherent to majority party leadership, regardless of the distribution of preferences in the chamber. Party leaders may use these powers to bestow benefits on members who are particularly supportive of party positions. Leaders may also choose to impose penalties on disobedient members, though they do so only rarely because they will almost certainly seek to obtain the support of those members on future votes (Sinclair 1983).

In addition to the unqualified powers of the majority party, the conditional party government theory (e.g., Rohde 1991, Aldrich 1995, Aldrich and Rohde 1997–98) holds that a broader range of powers may be granted to party leadership when the preferences of the membership of the respective political parties are internally homogeneous and when the parties are ideologically distinct from each other. Indeed, proponents of the conditional party government theory contend that these conditional powers are granted to party leaders for the express purpose of promoting party unity.

While these two predominant theories of party influence differ in important respects, both allow for party leaders to exert influence on their members by making exchanges that are mutually advantageous to the party and to the individual member. This is particularly explicit in the conditional party government approach, but Cox and McCubbins (2005) note that party leaders must regularly seek votes on the margin to pass legislation the party supports (even though it can use its powers of negative agenda control to prevent passage of legislation the party disapproves of). The commodities a party exchanges with its members may be either conditional upon the distribution of preferences within the chamber (in accordance with the conditional party government theory) or independent of preferences (more along the lines of party cartel theory, but potentially extending beyond negative agenda control). As such, an exchange theory of party influence can be seen as a complement to, rather than a rival hypothesis of, predominant theories of party influence. Indeed, in many ways an exchange theory of party influence completes existing theories of party influence by showing that parties have an avenue through which they may actively influence legislators to support party goals (as opposed to simply preventing them from supporting the opposing party). These avenues of influence need not be conditional on the distribution of preferences within the chamber.

Exchange theories have been applied widely in the social sciences. The roots of exchange theory were developed in sociology, with Homans (1958) arguing that social relationships can be evaluated in terms of what each party to a relationship gives and receives. In this conception, all social activities are an exchange of goods or intangibles, all of which have rewards and costs (Homans 1961: 12–13). The theory predicts that individuals required to give more than they receive from a relationship are likely to exit the relationship. Applications of this principle abound in political science, including the exchange theory of interest group membership (Salisbury 1969) and Waldman's (1972) applications of exchange theory to citizens' political activities (including political culture, legitimacy, and conflict resolution). Perhaps it is because the resurgence of congressional parties was just beginning as Waldman wrote that he did not discuss the application of exchange theory to political parties (especially party leaders) and their members as an important determinant of activity within Congress. Nevertheless, we will see that exchanges brokered by party leaders that help both members and parties further their goals will prove to be powerful sources of party influence.

We have already outlined the major ambitions of legislators (election to public office, power in Washington, and implementing good public policy), but exchange theory also requires us to consider the goals held by the parties. Political parties hold two fundamental goals. First, political parties aspire to control a country's governing institutions and to thereby manage the coercive power of government (Downs 1957). Second, political parties seek to enact their preferred policies. The idea of policy-oriented congressional parties goes as far back as Wilson (1885), but the goal is reiterated in contemporary works on parties as procedural coalitions (e.g., Cox and McCubbins 1993, 2005). In many ways, the goal of majority status is much like an individual legislator's goal of election: It is difficult for a party to craft good public policy without the power that comes with majority status. Nevertheless, it seems as unreasonable to think that parties have no goal but to control the government as it is unreasonable to think that politicians have no goal but to be elected. Indeed, the very reason why parties seek to control the government is so they can create what they deem to be good policy. A party derives few benefits from ruling if it cannot implement at least some of its preferred policies.

Drawing from exchange theory, I contend that political party leaders broker exchanges with party members that are crafted to help both parties and party members reach their respective goals. While a number of such exchanges likely exist, in the constraints of this project I consider just two: The exchange of contributions (from party leaders) for unity in roll-call voting (from party members) and the exchange of positions of power (from party leaders) for unity in roll-call voting and financial support of party goals.

Leadership Contributions and Members' Electoral Goals

If party leaders are able to offer financial support to help candidates to meet their electoral ambitions, those candidates will be willing to reciprocate by supporting party goals. Campaign contributions from party leaders are helpful to candidates on three levels. First, the money itself is necessary in order to wage a successful campaign (Jacobson 2004). The average competitive House campaign now costs over $600,000, and campaign costs continue to rise (Herrnson 2004). As the scramble for campaign funds increases in intensity, members look more and more to congressional party leaders for financial support. Consider the 2004 campaign in Louisiana's 7th Congressional District. Although this seat had never been held by a Republican, when incumbent representative Chris John left the House to seek a Senate seat, the leaders of both parties viewed this seat as "in play." Two Republicans and three Democrats ran in the nonpartisan primary that could, according to Louisiana law, decide the election if any one candidate received over 50% of the vote. The Democratic Party supported their candidates largely by making independent expenditures against the Republican candidates. In contrast, House Republicans channeled money from their PCCs and leadership PACs directly into the campaign of their preferred candidate, the heart surgeon Charles Boustany Jr., to the tune of about $200,000—more than Boustany's runoff opponent, State Senator Willie Mount, raised from all sources in the primary election. The massive amount of fund-raising assistance was particularly important because this was Boustany's first political campaign. After the primary, House Democrats rallied to Mount's cause, contributing over $100,000 from their PCCs and leadership PACs. Member contributions made up nearly 15% of Boustany's fund-raising and about 10% of Mount's receipts. Ultimately receiving over $300,000 in contributions from fellow Republicans, Boustany won the election.

Second, contributions from party leaders can serve as the "seed money" that is necessary so as to get other fund-raising activities under way. Major fund-raising techniques require certain levels of start-up funds. Without some initial funding, candidates are almost certainly destined for failure. Funds from party leaders proved to be critical for Shelly Moore Capito in her 2000 bid to take a West Virginia congressional seat that had been a safe seat for Democrats until Bob Wise retired after the 106th Congress. Capito's opponent was a wealthy lawyer who had self-financed his $3.5 million campaign to win the primary election. Capito needed money just to get into the race. Republican members of Congress and their leadership PACs provided about one-third of the start-up money she raised to get her campaign off the ground (Bedlington and Malbin 2003). Capito used this seed money to organize a campaign that went on to raise over $2.5 million and defeated her opponent. She continues to represent that same West Virginia district today.

Finally, contributions from party leaders act as a signal of quality to other donors. Potential contributors are more willing to back candidates when party leaders have already endorsed the candidate with a leadership PAC or PCC contribution. Because contributions from party leaders lead to additional contributions from non-party sources, the actual value of leadership PAC and PCC contributions is much greater than their raw dollar amount. Glasgow (1998, 2002) exemplifies this point for party committee contributions with a formal model and empirical test. It seems that a similar effect would apply for leadership PAC and PCC contributions. In the case of Representative Capito, Bedlington and Malbin (2003) note that the early contributions from party leaders signaled to donors in the Republican network that Capito had a real chance to win and was worth supporting. The value of these party contributions was multiplied as they led to more and more support.

Member Contributions, Party Unity, and the Goal of Power in Washington

In addition to helping members meet their electoral goals, parties can help members achieve power in Washington. Parties seek monetary support for their candidates and voting support for the party's agenda. They may be willing to offer positions of power to members of Congress who are willing to support the party both financially and ideologically. Heberlig (2003) shows that parties reward members who contribute to party causes by granting their requests for seats on prestigious committees. However, scholars have not yet firmly determined how voting unity and fund-raising capacity affect the selection of many other influential positions in the House, including committee and subcommittee chairs. If parties establish ideological and pecuniary support benchmarks for leadership candidates, they may be able to induce members of Congress who seek power in Washington to support the financial and policy goals of the party.

The 2004 race for Senate minority leader shows that financial support may be, in some instances, even more important than ideology. As a pro-life Mormon, the moderate Senator Harry Reid (D-NV) seems a little out of place with his fellow Senate Democrats. Yet, when Minority Leader Tom Daschle lost his seat in the 2004 election, Reid threw his hat into the ring as a candidate for the leader of his party in the Senate. Christopher Dodd (D-CT) challenged him. As ideology goes, few would argue that Dodd is a poor fit to his party. Yet, Reid won the race. While Reid's service as minority whip was clearly a factor in his ascension to the helm of the Senate Democrats, he had also been working quietly for years as a prolific contributor to the Democratic Party and to Democratic candidates. In the six years (three election cycles) prior to becoming minority leader, Reid gave about $1,700,000 to other candidates and to Democratic Party committees from his personal campaign funds and another $700,000 from his leadership PAC. In contrast, Dodd gave only about $500,000 during the same period of time. Reid's remarkable fund-raising capacity seemed to compensate for his ideological incompatibility with his party and carried him to victory in the Senate minority leader race.

The party's willingness to make leadership positions conditional on member contributions offers at least a partial solution to the collective action problem the political parties face in soliciting support from their members. To the extent that party leaders control who holds positions of power in Congress (i.e., committee chairs, subcommittee chairs, and party leadership positions), they may use them as a selective incentive to encourage members to support the party and party candidates. While other potential selective incentives exist, these seem to be particularly important in encouraging members of Congress to financially support their parties.[3]

Discussion

The ambition-based exchange framework introduced here unites knowledge from research in campaign finance, parties, elections, and Congress to explain how parties enter exchanges with members of Congress to encourage support of party goals. In the instances discussed here, member contributions are the currency exchanged by at least one side of the deal (the member or the party) for something from the other side. This approach does not negate either the conditional party government or party cartel theories of party influence. Rather, it largely works within the context of these existing theories of party influence. The approach introduced here adds depth to these theories by connecting the power of political parties back to the electoral process. The exchanges involving member contributions discussed in this book may simply be viewed as additional avenues that allow party leaders to exercise influence in addition to the procedural and institutional powers considered in most discussions of party strength.

This establishes the theoretical framework for this study—Party leaders in Congress help candidates to satisfy their ambitions, and party members reciprocate by supporting the goals of their party. A multitude of possible hypotheses exist regarding exchanges between parties and party members. Rather than attempting to explore them all, I limit myself to the evaluation of just three hypotheses to illustrate the exchange framework as it applies to member contributions. First, I consider the hypothesis that members who receive campaign contributions from their party leaders reciprocate by casting roll-call votes in support of party leadership. Then I evaluate the hypothesis that members who support the party (both financially and with voting unity) are more likely to win committee and subcommittee chair positions. Finally I investigate the notion that members of Congress campaigning for core party leadership positions are more likely to succeed when they make large contributions to their party and to fellow party candidates. With these basic hypotheses now in place, and a general rationale for why they may be true, we now turn to tests of these hypotheses.

CHAPTER 4

Leadership Investment in Legislative Loyalty in the U.S. House

From a comparative perspective, political parties in the United States are quite weak (Ware 1996). Nevertheless, history demonstrates that the relative strength of American parties waxes and wanes over time. After a period of relative weakness through the mid-twentieth century, American congressional parties have experienced a remarkable resurgence of strength. This revival of congressional party influence has attracted the attention of political scientists, and many explanations have been offered for this resurgence. Some scholars have gone beyond the recent upsurge to offer more general theories of the dynamics of partisan strength.

Applying the exchange framework proposed in chapter 3, I contend here that party leaders can gain influence with members of Congress by helping members to realize their ambitions. This chapter advances the notion that party leaders who help support candidates in their campaigns for election or reelection receive returns on their investment in the form of party voting. This approach is unique in that rather than looking exclusively for institutional roots of party strength, it allows us to consider possible electoral origins for party strength. As noted previously, this has the benefit of tying together research in campaign finance, parties, elections, and Congress to make a connection between the electoral process and congressional voting behavior.

Institutional Studies of Party Unity

Given the minimal strength of political parties in the mid-twentieth century, scholars devoted little time to studying party leadership. Cooper and Brady (1981) note that the Speakers of the House in this era were not necessarily weak because they were poor leaders, but rather because the historical and institutional context did not allow for strong leadership tactics. Nevertheless, Ripley (1969) noted that party leaders had at least some power, though it was dependent on the partisan composition of Congress, the party in the White House, and the president's attitude toward his legislative responsibilities. Sinclair (1983) wrote in a different world—the congressional reforms of the 1970s showed that liberal Democrats could pull together a winning coalition with greater party discipline than had marked the lengthy era of committee chair "barons." This trend continued, and as party leaders gained in strength, scholars like Rohde (1991) and Cox and McCubbins (1993) began to offer explanations for the growth in party unity.

Cox and McCubbins's (1993, 2005) party cartel theory holds that certain institutional powers, particularly agenda control, give the majority party significant power over legislative outcomes. The unique claim advanced most clearly in Cox and McCubbins (2005) is that majority party leaders do not need to ask members of Congress to vote with the party on final passage. Rather, by using their procedural advantages (and by asking members for their votes on procedural matters), they ensure that the only bills that come up for a vote are those where the party will win its desired outcome.

While a second approach to party influence, the conditional party government theory (Rohde 1991; Aldrich 1995; Aldrich and Rohde 1997–98, 2000), acknowledges that the majority party wields significant institutional powers, they contend that the amount of power that members are willing to delegate to party leaders will be greatest when the two political parties are ideologically distant from one another (inter-party polarization) and internally cohesive (intra-party homogeneity). Finocchiaro and Rohde (2002) argue that even the powers of agenda control (which are central to the party cartel theory) are conditional upon the distribution of preferences within parties and within the chamber. When the two conditions are better met, however, party members will be willing to cede even more powers to the leadership.

The debate on party strength intensified in the wake of a challenge from Krehbiel (1993). He claims that while the roll-call voting patterns of members of Congress may be consistent with their party identification, these votes are motivated by the ideological preferences of the constituency rather than the activities of party leaders. Krehbiel argues that "significant party behavior" only occurs when members vote with their party when they would have voted otherwise if motivated solely by their constituency.

In Krehbiel's wake, a host of scholars have mobilized to show that political parties and party leaders indeed exert significant influence on members of Congress. One set of these studies consists of empirically based work whose only goal is to demonstrate that parties affect the roll-call voting behavior of members of Congress. Nokken (2000) examines members who switch political parties. While these members have the same constituency before and after their switch, they are subject to a different set of party pressures. Nokken's results show that members who switch parties change their roll-call voting behavior even though their constituency remains the same. Along similar lines,

Den Hartog (2005) shows that senators' roll rates (the frequency with which they voted against a bill but it still passed) shifted when Vermont Senator Jim Jeffords left the Republican Party and control of the Senate shifted from the Republicans to the Democrats. Other work compares legislatures that have party structures with nonpartisan legislatures (Jenkins 1999, Aldrich and Battista 2002), showing that parties play an important role in structuring legislators' voting behavior. Notwithstanding the strength of the evidence in these studies, they do not explain why parties are able to exert such influence. That is, while data establish that parties affect how legislators vote, the mechanisms by which parties exert this influence are not clear.

A second set of studies in response to Krehbiel's work goes beyond simple empiricism to offer a theoretical framework for party influence in addition to empirical evidence. These works (e.g., Cox and McCubbins 1994, Dion and Huber 1996, Cox and McCubbins 1997, Aldrich and Rohde 2000) largely build on the party cartel or conditional party government approaches. While they differ somewhat in their approach and in their evidence, they have one particularly important factor in common: They argue that party strength arises largely from institutional features of Congress.

Still, recent work has suggested that the "permanent" powers touted by the party cartel approach are limited to negative agenda control (Cox and McCubbins 2005, Finocchiaro and Rohde 2002). Notwithstanding the significance of that power, party leaders are not only interested in blocking legislation they dislike; they are also clearly interested in passing certain pieces of legislation. What tools do party leaders have at their disposal to ensure that legislation they favor succeeds?

Conditional party government theorists contend that additional institutional powers to help further majority party success come as the aforementioned twin conditions of conditional party government are increasingly realized. Nevertheless, in the presence of a homogenous majority that is distant from the minority party, majority legislation will be likely to succeed even without institutional powers. Indeed, it is when the distribution of preferences in the chamber is not favorable to party success that parties most need institutional tools to further party goals in spite of a heterogeneous majority.

In contrast to party cartel and conditional party government approaches to party strength, I contend that parties will best be able to exert influence on the voting behavior of their members when they further the political ambitions of their members. Given the primacy of the electoral goal, party leaders could potentially gain large returns by offering campaign support in exchange for voting loyalty. This does not imply that the two dominant approaches to congressional party influence are incorrect or inappropriate. Indeed, the existence of exchanges between party leaders does not negate the validity of either the party cartel approach or the conditional party government hypothesis. However, this ambition-based exchange theory suggests an additional avenue through which parties may exercise influence. In contrast to the dominant theories of party strength that are generally based on institutional powers, I demonstrate that at least a portion of party strength grows from the electoral process.

Electoral Roots of Party Influence

A few scholars have hypothesized that electoral support from the party could result in increased party unity. Herrnson (1986) noted that even in the age of candidate-centered campaigns, assistance from the party can play a significant role in a congressional campaign. Indeed, parties play a crucial role in assisting candidates to win congressional seats—from the simple lending of a party "brand name" (Aldrich 1995) to candidate nominations, free campaign consultants, and in some instances, substantial amounts of campaign funds (Herrnson 2004, Glasgow 2002).

Cantor and Herrnson (1997) and Damore and Hansford (1999) study the allocation of party funding (e.g., contributions from the NRCC or DCCC) to congressional candidates. Looking across multiple years and across both political parties, they find very little support for the idea that party campaign committees contribute more money to the legislators with the best voting record.

Studying elections to state legislatures, however, Gierzynski (1992) found that while contributions from party committees were not correlated with voting unity, contributions from leadership PACs run by state legislators seemed to be correlated with party unity. Party committees, it seems, act as seat maximizers, simply working toward gaining or maintaining a majority. Ideology is not central to their mission—as Tom Reynolds, former chair of the Republican Congressional Campaign Committee put it. "I don't let any issue become a litmus test or barrier in building a Republican coalition" (Republican Mainstreet Partnership 2003, 4).

In contrast, congressional party leaders are engaged in the daily battle for the 218 votes needed to pass a bill in the House. Thus, party leaders have a strong incentive to allocate their funds in a manner that not only maximizes seats, but that also promotes party unity within the chamber (Gierzynski 1992). The theoretical framework developed in chapter 3 explains that candidates will be most willing to support party goals when party leaders help candidates to meet their electoral ambitions. More specifically, when party leaders make campaign contributions to further the electoral ambition of party candidates, those candidates will be willing to reciprocate by supporting party goals.

The Logic of the Money-Votes Connection

The task that remains before examining the data is considering why a member of Congress would exchange their votes for campaign funds. Congressional scholars have devoted tremendous time and effort to studying the possible relationship between interest group campaign contributions and roll-call voting in Congress. The results of these inquiries can be summarized rather simply—there is little (if any) direct evidence that campaign contributions have a general effect on the way in which members of Congress vote. Chappell (1982) and Grenzke (1989) demonstrate that while there is a correlation between interest group campaign contributions to members of Congress and how those members vote, that correlation exists because groups contribute to members who already agree with them. Wawro (2001) exploits the temporal nature of votes and labor union contributions and again finds that campaign contributions do not change legislators' votes.

Two common explanations exist explaining why no relationship exists between campaign contributions and votes. First, members of Congress need the support of their constituency to ensure their reelection; offering votes "for sale" without regard for the constituency thus makes little sense. Second, the amounts of campaign contributions are so minimal ($5,000 per PAC per election, $1,000 per individual per election, but increased to $2,000 for individuals and all limits are indexed to inflation beginning in 2004) in the context of expensive, modern campaigns that a single campaign contribution doesn't make enough difference to a campaign to entice legislators to change their votes. While acknowledging the validity of these claims in many circumstances, I contend that neither of these criticisms applies well in the specific instance of contributions from congressional party leaders.

The Problem of the Constituency

In terms of a legislator maximizing their probability of reelection, the cost of a legislator voting with the party and against their constituency will often far exceed the value of a campaign contribution. Indeed, Carson (2005) shows that candidates sometimes defect from their party on salient issues to avoid the entrance of a challenger in the next election and thus to ensure their reelection. Nevertheless, in certain instances, members of Congress may find it in their interest to enter these exchanges with party leaders.

There are clearly some votes that are so important to a legislator's constituency that a rational legislator would not exchange his or her vote for any amount of campaign support. Indeed, party leaders would not want their members to risk their seat for a single vote on a single piece of legislation because doing so could jeopardize the party's chances of gaining/maintaining majority status. Nevertheless, a large number of votes exist where the legislator may gain more utility from entering into exchanges with party leaders. Many scholars have shown that party leaders effectively offer incentives to get their members to act in certain ways (e.g., Sinclair 1983, Cox and McCubbins 1993, Pearson 2005). While scholars have not considered leadership contributions as a means of ensuring voting unity, leadership contributions potentially fit into the set of tools that congressional leaders have for encouraging partisan roll-call voting.

The Problem of Small Contributions

A second reason why one may doubt the influence of campaign contributions is that the size of contributions allowed by law is quite small relative to the amount that candidates raise and spend in their campaigns. While it is true that the amount of an individual leadership contribution is relatively small, party leaders may contribute from both their personal campaign funds and from a leadership PAC. Then, when one multiplies these "double" contributions across the set of party leaders, the total amount becomes quite substantial (some candidates receive nearly 10 percent of their funds just from the top four leaders of their party). Particularly in competitive races, where every dollar counts, assistance from party leaders is very valuable to members of Congress.

In chapter 2, we noted that the amount of money passed into campaigns in this way has grown substantially over time. In the modern political landscape, the leadership PACs sponsored by a party leader may donate as much as (or even more than) the most active interest group or corporate PAC. Further, chapter 2 shows that much of this money comes from congressional leaders.

Moreover, even when the dollar amount of leadership contributions seems small relative to overall campaign expenditures, these contributions have importance beyond their face monetary value. Glasgow (1998, 2002) demonstrates that party campaign contributions may signal certain qualities about a candidate (especially ideology and willingness to work with party leaders) that assist him or her in tapping into a party's larger fund-raising network. A simple extension of those results would suggest that contributions from party leaders function in the same way. Glasgow notes that these contributions signal in part the candidate's ability to win a seat. Some may dispute the role of ideology in this process, as a party leader would virtually always support a member of their own party to occupy a seat in Congress over a member of the other party. Nevertheless, because party leaders must allocate limited resources, they are often forced to choose between supporting someone who would reciprocate with loyal voting (to the extent allowed by his or her constituency) and a member who would continue to pursue a moderate path. In those cases, the party leader's interests would clearly be served by supporting the candidate who will support the party.

Hypotheses and Data

Given the possibility of the relationship between leadership contributions and member voting, a rigorous empirical investigation of the question is merited. The dependent variable for this analysis will be *Party Unity* scores (as calculated by *Congressional Quarterly*) for members who served three or more consecutive terms continuously from the 102nd to 106th Congresses.[1] These scores indicate the percentage of the time a member votes with his or her party when a majority of one party votes against a majority of the other party. The average party unity score in this time period is 84.

The primary independent variables of interest are based on contributions from party committees and from party leaders to members of Congress. First, I include *Party Contributions*, the amount of money that a legislator receives from political party committees (e.g., the NRCC and DCCC). This includes direct party expenditures, party independent expenditures, and party-coordinated expenditures. Previous work has shown that party committees are simply interested in maximizing the number of seats their party holds (Kuhn 1999, Gierzynski 1992). As a result, parties donate to any member of the party who could benefit from this contribution, without regard for party unity scores. This "something for everyone" approach is borne out by the data—over 90 percent of members in the sample received money from their party, with an average contribution of $9,439.

While previous research has suggested that there is no.relationship between party committee contributions and roll-call voting, party leaders who make contributions to other members of Congress may use a different strategy for distributing funds. Because leaders seek voting support from party members while also trying to maximize the number of seats their party holds, they may treat their contributions as investments upon which the receiving members should offer returns in terms of voting loyalty. I measure *Leadership Contributions* as the amount of money that members of Congress receive from the top four leaders of their party.[2] These leaders tend to donate most of their funds through their leadership PACs, but frequently supplement those contributions with donations from their PCCs. In the 102nd–106th Congresses, about 50 percent of members of Congress received contributions from at least one leader in their last election. Those who benefited from leadership funding received an average of $4,675. When financial contribution variables for parties and party leaders are entered into the model, they are logged to model diminishing marginal returns on contributions (Jacobson 1980).

The direction of causality for leadership contributions is questionable, though. As with all studies of campaign contributions and votes, it is possible that leaders simply allocate their funds to those who are already staunch partisans. This would result in a correlation between money and votes, yet the money is clearly not the motivating factor in voting behavior. A solution to this problem will be addressed in the following section.

Beyond contributions, legislators engaged in a competitive election may find a need to respond more to the needs of their constituencies in the next Congress in order to enhance their chances for continued reelection. To estimate the effect of district competitiveness on party unity, I include *Competitiveness*, coded as a legislator's margin of victory over the next closest candidate.

Because district preferences naturally have a substantial effect on the way in which legislators vote (see, e.g., Kingdon 1989) these preferences must be accounted for in the model. A diverse literature addresses several ways to measure district preferences (e.g., Miller and Stokes 1963; Kalt and Zupan 1984; Erikson and Wright 1980; Levendusky, Pope, and Jackman 2005). However, given that the bulk of the evidence suggests little or no meaningful change over time in district preferences (see especially Levendusky, Pope, and Jackman 2005 for strong evidence using a very sophisticated approach), we can control for district preferences using a fixed-effects model (see the appendix for statistical details).

Statistical Model and Results

An Instrumental Variables Approach

Due to the possible endogeneity problem with leadership contributions and party loyalty, I estimate both a standard fixed-effects (FE) model and a fixed-effects two-stage least squares (FE2SLS) model. As the name implies, the latter

TABLE 4.1 Fixed-Effects and FE2SLS Models of Party Unity

	Fixed-Effects	FE2SLS
	Coefficient (Std. Err.)	Coefficient (Std. Err.)
Leadership Contributions	.206* (.076)	.579* (.21)
Party Contributions	−.072 (.082)	−.168 (.099)
Victory Margin	.038* (.010)	.037* (.010)
Joint Significance of Coefficients (Sig.)	$F = 7.65$ $p < .001$	$\chi^2 = 352{,}934$ $p < .001$
Joint F-test of Fixed Effects (Sig.)	16.26 $p < .001$	15.33 $p < .001$
χ^2 Test of Overidentifying Restrictions (Sig.)	—	.132 $p = .716$
Davidson-MacKinnon Exogeneity Test (Sig.)	—	3.703 $p < .0549$
Observations (Groups)	828 (395)	828 (395)

NOTE: Dependent variable is party unity scores.

*Denotes $p < .05$, one-tailed.

SOURCES: FEC and Center for Responsive Politics.

FIGURE 4.1 Party Unity Increase from Leadership Contributions

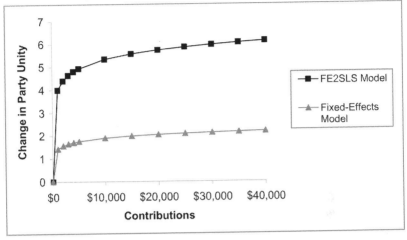

estimator is the fixed-effects analog of the standard two-stage least squares estimator. Details on the instruments used and tests regarding assumptions about the strength and validity of the instruments are contained in the statistical appendix for this chapter.

The Davidson and MacKinnon (1993) test of exogeneity tests the hypothesis that a regular fixed-effects estimator is consistent (i.e., whatever endogeneity may be present does not distort the fixed-effects results and thus the two-stage least squares estimator is unnecessary). The test for the exogeneity of leadership contributions very narrowly fails to reject the null hypothesis that leadership contributions are exogenous ($p = .0549$, with .05 being the usual cutoff). However, with the results of the test being so close to the standard cutoff, presenting the results of both models seems to be a prudent way to assuage any lingering concerns about endogeneity. The results from both models are listed in Table 4.1.

Across both models, the results are quite similar. The most important result is that contributions from party leaders have a strong, significant effect on roll-call voting behavior. Because leadership contributions are logged, a graphic depiction of the relationship between contributions and changes in loyalty eases the interpretation of these coefficients. Figure 4.1 shows that the first $5,000 in leadership contributions yields, on average, an increase of 1.7 to 5 points in party unity (depending on whether one uses the FE2SLS or fixed-effects results). An additional $15,000 in contributions creates about another one-point increase, with further increases yielding only minimal increases in loyalty.

In contrast to leadership PACs, the analysis shows that money from party committees does not have any significant effect on party loyalty. Our original expectations anticipated this result as party committees simply want to maximize the seats they hold in Congress. The result (that party committee contributions are not related to party unity scores) is consistent with the idea that the party committees indeed donate indiscriminately to party members with no expectation of a return on the investment. Thus, legislators offer no loyalty in reward for party committee support. This finding is consistent with the theoretical expectations expressed in previous research on party committee contributions (Kuhn 1999). Finally, the models show that candidates who face less competitive elections (larger victory margins) display somewhat higher levels of party unity. This may be because some members face less pressure from their constituency and are thus free to pursue party interests.

A Time-Based Approach

Wawro (2001) makes an important statistical contention regarding the use of instrumental variables to make claims regarding campaign contributions and legislators' votes. While resolving correlations between an independent variable and the error term deals with the statistical problems of endogeneity (bias and inconsistency), Wawro notes that this does not necessarily establish the direction of causality. An alternative approach is to use information about the timing of contributions and changes in loyalty to establish the fact that contributions directly influence votes (as opposed to leaders simply contributing to members who already have high levels of party unity). By comparing party unity before and after leadership contributions are made, we can assess more intuitively whether contributions affect votes. Unless one believes that leaders are somehow able to divine in advance which members are going to increase their voting unity and that they contribute exclusively to those members, the endogeneity problem can be avoided by considering *changes* in party unity. If those who receive contributions from their leaders have higher increases in party unity from one Congress to the next than those who do not receive them, we would have evidence that leadership contributions increase party unity. Table 4.2 shows that the average changes in party unity for individuals who received contributions from their leaders was 1.21 points while party unity actually decreased by an average of .03 among those who did not receive contributions. A difference of means test shows that this difference is statistically significant ($p < .01$, two-tailed).

Beyond this simple and intuitive test, estimating a regression model (more specifically a fixed-effects model) with changes in unity as the dependent variable allows us to assess the effect of different sizes of leadership contributions (rather than simply considering whether such contributions were received or not as we did in Table 4.2) and further allows us to control for other determinants of party unity used in this model (Table 4.1).[3] The results of this fixed-effects model appear in Table 4.3. The results are substantively

TABLE 4.2 Mean Changes in Party Unity by Receipt of Leadership Contributions

	Received Some Contribution	Received No Contribution
Mean Change in Party Unity from One Congress to the Next	1.23	−.03
n	580	1,202

NOTE: Based on leadership PAC and PCC contributions from the top four leaders of each party and party unity in the 101st–106th Congresses. A difference of means test finds statistical significance ($p < .01$, two-tailed).

SOURCE: Federal Elections Commission

similar to the results of the models in Table 4.1,[4] showing that leadership contributions results in significant increases in party unity scores even when controlling for other factors. Party contributions, as in the previous model, have no effect on party unity.

TABLE 4.3 Fixed-Effects Model of Changes in Party Unity

	Coefficient (Std. Err.)
Leadership Contributions	.223* (.086)
Party Contributions	.008 (.091)
Victory Margin	.020* (.011)
Joint F-test of Fixed Effects (Sig.)	.70 $p > .10$
Observations (Groups)	1774 (664)

NOTE: Dependent variable concerns changes in party unity.

*Denotes $p < .05$, one-tailed.

Discussion

In the end, we find strong evidence that leadership financial support significantly increases the partisan loyalty of legislators. The statistical techniques employed address the endogeneity issues endemic to campaign finance research to show that contributions from party leaders increase party unity in the House of Representatives. While many studies have struggled to show that campaign contributions affect roll-call voting, these results show that party leaders allocate their personal campaign resources to increase the unity of their party. While other studies of campaign contributions and votes have generally not found a relationship, this research shows that party leaders are uniquely positioned to use campaign contributions as a tool to encourage legislators to support the party's preferred positions. The results suggest that there are limits on how much legislators will change their voting behavior, but they are equally clear that leaders' investments yield small but significant returns.

The results suggest that the ideal strategy for leaders would be to give relatively small amounts of money to a large number of legislators. Given that the effects of leadership contributions level out after about $15,000 in contributions, party leaders are better off spreading contributions across many legislators rather than concentrating larger sums of money on a few candidates. This quick leveling off may result from the fact that legislators are constrained by the preferences of their district in their voting behavior, and may only be able to marginally increase their party unity while keeping their district satisfied.

While party leaders can effectively increase loyalty, it appears that party committees do not receive a return on their investment in terms of increased party unity. Given the results of previous research, this result is not surprising. Party committees operate on the assumption that any party member is better than a member of the opposing party. Thus, they donate without an expectation of increased loyalty. This is not to say that party committee contributions are unimportant—the number of seats held by party members is certainly a matter of concern. However, it is clear that party committees and party leaders operate with different goals and strategies, and thus achieve different results from their contributions.

The Exchange Theory and Other Theories of Party Influence

The evidence presented here has profound implications for theories of partisan influence. The conditional party government theory holds that party leaders wield the greatest influence when legislators' preferences are polarized between parties and are homogeneous within parties. These findings show that enterprising congressional leaders can use contributions to congressional candidates (a feature of the electoral process) to build their influence with party members.

When leaders offer financial support to members' reelection campaigns, those members respond with higher levels of party unity.

The party cartel theory of partisan influence emphasizes negative agenda control as an unconditional power of the majority party in the U.S. House. This being the case, it may seem that party leaders would not need to encourage loyalty. However, the unconditional powers outlined in Cox and McCubbins (2005) are limited to negative agenda control, but say less about the positive powers of the majority (the ability to pass legislation the majority supports). As a result, Cox and McCubbins (2005) concede that party leaders must still regularly seek votes on the margin. Leadership contributions to other members are one way in which leaders work to obtain these votes.

These results support the theoretical framework developed in chapter 3, showing that when party leaders help members to realize their ambitions, members reciprocate by helping the party reach its goals. This chapter establishes the fact that leaders are able to strengthen legislative parties by raising and contributing money to other candidates and thus supporting their electoral ambitions. Still, once members of Congress have secured reelection, they may turn toward achieving other goals—particularly, as Fenno (1973) noted, power in Washington and good public policy. In chapter 5, we address how the member-contributor phenomenon shapes exchanges between party leaders and members who seek to achieve these two goals by becoming committee leaders in the U.S. House.

Statistical Appendix

Given that the data consist of multiple legislators observed over several time periods, the basic model is given by the standard panel data model,

$$y_{it} = x_{it}\beta + \alpha_i + u_{it}$$

where i indexes members of Congress, t indexes time (in Congresses), y_{it} is the dependent variable (party unity), β is a vector of coefficients, x_{it} is a vector of explanatory variables, α_i is a vector of unit-specific effects, and u_{it} is the disturbance term. The most commonly used estimators for the panel model are the fixed-effects and random-effects models. The fixed-effects estimator is guaranteed to be consistent but can be inefficient, while the random-effects estimator is more efficient but not always consistent. A Hausman test comparing the fixed- and random-effects estimators rejects the null hypothesis that the coefficients are equal, leading us to choose the consistent fixed-effects model. A Hausman test of a random-effects two-stage least squares model against the FE2SLS model similarly rejects the null, pointing to the FE2SLS model.

For the interested reader, the first-stage results appear in Table 4.4. The results show that the two instruments, leadership contributions lagged one time period and leadership contributions lagged two time periods, are sufficiently strong for estimation of the model. This is reflected in statistical tests of the strength of the instruments—the partial r^2 is greater than .1, and the value of the partial F test exceeds 10. Thus, we can proceed with confidence that the selected instruments are sufficiently strong to obtain correct results.

TABLE 4.4 First-Stage Estimates for the FE2SLS Model

	Coefficient (Std. Err.)
Party Committee Contributions	.245* (.047)
Victory Margin	−.005 (.006)
Leadership Contributions at t-1	−.330* (.042)
Leadership Contributions at t-2	−.163* (.040)
Partial r^2 for Instruments	.133
Partial F for Instruments	33.03 ($p < .001$)
Observations (Groups)	828 (395)

NOTE: *Denotes $p < .05$, two-tailed.

CHAPTER 5

Member Contributions and the Politics of House Committee Chair Selection

Throughout the history of Congress, committees have been a significant feature of congressional organization. Wilson's (1885) statement has become conventional wisdom—Congress at work is Congress in committee. The power that party leaders exercise over committees, however, continues to be a dynamic feature of Congress. If party leaders can control the committee chair selection process, they have a powerful incentive to offer in exchange for the loyalty of party members who seek committee leadership positions. Recent history suggests that the power pendulum is swinging from committee leadership back toward party leaders. Since Republicans took control of Congress in 1994, the norm of seniority (where the most senior member of a committee has a veritable property right to a committee chair position) has been violated with increasing frequency. Have party leaders successfully gained control of the committee chair selection process? If so, what role might member-to-member and member-to-party contributions play in a party-dominated chair selection process? An example may be illustrative.

John Boehner (R-OH) is a Republican who works hard for his party, a fact illustrated by his victory in the race to succeed Tom DeLay as House majority leader (in the Democratic-controlled 110th Congress he serves as minority leader). After easily winning reelection in 2000, Boehner sought to increase his profile in the House of Representatives by obtaining a committee chair position on the House Committee on Education and the Workforce. The previous chair, Bill Goodling (R-PA) had been forced to step down by the six-year term limits placed in committee chairs in the 104th Congress. Boehner had only served two years on the Education Committee, but he was counting on the statements by Republican Party leaders to the effect that that seniority was to be only one factor among many in determining who would chair each committee. Boehner hoped that his solid conservative credentials and prolific

51

fund-raising (over $550,000 given to Republican Party committees and Republican candidates in the 2000 election cycle) would carry him to victory. By traditional standards, Thomas Petri's (R-WI) twenty-two years of service on the committee would have guaranteed him the chair position, even though he only donated about $1,000 in support of party causes. When the Republican Steering Committee voted, they rewarded fund-raising more than seniority, and the gavel went to Boehner.

The ability of party leaders to exchange committee chair positions for money depends on their ability to control the committee chair selection process. Yet, throughout most of the twentieth century, the ability of party leaders to influence the chair selection process was minimal because of the seniority system (Abram and Cooper 1968; Polsby, Gallaher, and Rundquist 1969). In this chapter, I will discuss the rise of the seniority system and its implications for committee chair selection. Then I show that, consistent with the conditional party government theory, as parties became more cohesive, party members granted increasing control of committee chair selection to the party, even allowing party leaders to abandon the seniority system. Instead, as predicted by the exchange theory, party leaders established a system that favors candidates who raise funds and who then "share the wealth" with their respective parties and with fellow-party candidates. The chapter concludes with a discussion of the implications of these findings for theories of congressional organization.

The Rise (and Decline) of the Seniority System in the U.S. House of Representatives

The Czar Era

Textbook versions of committee system evolution typically begin at the height of party power in the 1890–1910 era. Speaker-czars such as Thomas Reed (R-ME) and Joseph Cannon (R-IL) ran a tight ship, and members of the party "crew" who stepped out of line were quickly thrown overboard. Rather than being repositories of power that could be used to counter the wishes of party leadership, committees were simply tools of the speaker. In the czar era, committee chairs were handpicked by the Speaker and committee chairs who flinched in their loyalty were removed from their positions. In this way, Speakers were able to tightly control the activities of committee chairs. Writing in this era, Wilson (1885) noted that although ideological proximity to the Speaker was the key factor in selecting chairs, Speakers did select the most senior party member on the committee where feasible. It is also further worth noting that once a Speaker has placed his ideal chair in power, there is no need for additional seniority violations. The influence of seniority in this era (relative to later history) can be seen in Figure 5.1, which shows the proportion of committee chair appointments in each year that constitute uncompensated violations of seniority.[1]

FIGURE 5.1 Proportion of Uncompensated Seniority Violations in Committee Chair Appointments, 1889-1957

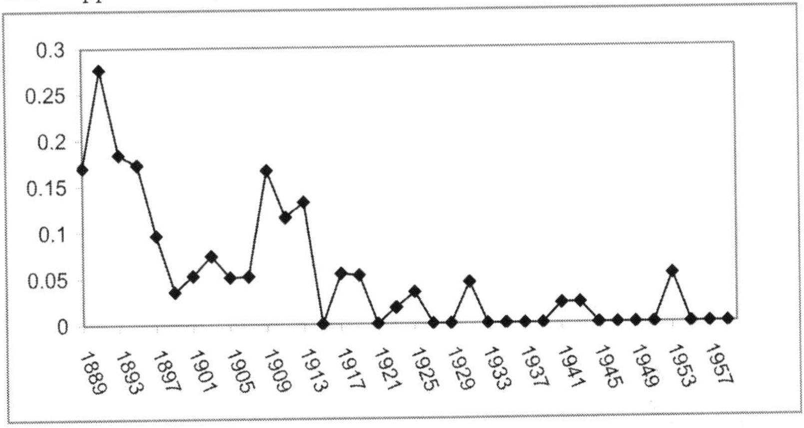

SOURCE: Polsby, Gallaher, and Rundquist (1969).

The graph shows that throughout the czar era, violations were fairly common, but never did more than about one-third of committee chair appointments in a single year violate seniority.

Eventually, some members of Congress found the constraints of strong party leadership more than they could bear. A coalition of Democrats and insurgent Republicans "revolted" against Cannon and stripped the speakership of many of its powers. Among the reforms was a requirement that all committee slots (members and chairs) were subject to election rather than to an unquestioned appointment by the Speaker. This and other reforms led to a gradual transition of power from the Speaker to party caucuses and eventually to committee chairs (Sala 2003; Brady, Cooper, and Hurley 1979). Through the transitional era, a norm developed where the member of the majority party with the longest service on a committee was simply entitled to chair that committee. While different scholars designate the end of this transitional period with different dates, in Figure 5.1 one can clearly see that as history moved from the czar era to the era of strong committee chairs (beginning sometime in the late 1930s or 1940s), that uncompensated seniority violations essentially disappear.

Era of Strong Committee Chairs

If Speakers from the Cannon/Reed era were accurately referred to as czars, then common parlance referring to committee chairs after the transitional period as *barons* is certainly an apt term. Committee chairs in this era possessed expansive powers, including agenda setting, proxy voting, and gatekeeping. Because of the seniority norm, these powers were delegated based on length of service rather than

on ideology. Nevertheless, selection by the seniority system was not without ideological consequences. Hinckley (1971) notes long-serving legislators from the
one-party South obtained a disproportionate number of committee chair positions
through the mid-twentieth century. Regional cleavages in the Democratic Party
had existed at least since the New Deal, but debates over civil rights through the
1950s and 1960s made the divide particularly pervasive and pernicious.

Post-Reform Era

Consistent with the predictions of conditional party government theory, shifts in
the distribution of preferences in the Democratic Party (especially southern Democrats) led to a shift in power back toward the party. A coalition of northeastern
liberals known as the Democratic Study Group (DSG) banded together to consider reforms that would remove power from conservative southern committee
chairs. Based on arguments pushed by DSG members, a number of institutional
reforms were enacted. Among them was a 1971 initiative that allowed the Democratic Committee on Committees to recommend a committee chair who was not
the most senior member of the committee. Further, the caucus began to vote yea
or nay on individual committee chairs instead of simultaneously approving or dis-
approving the entire list (Rohde 1991). These and other reforms in this era began
to transfer power from committee chairs back into the hands of party leaders.

FIGURE 5.2 Proportion of Uncompensated Seniority Violations in Committee
Chair Appointments, 1947–2007

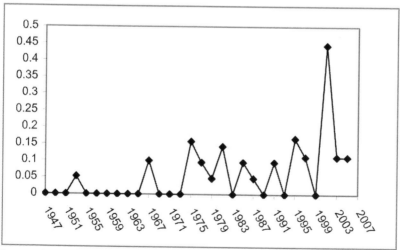

SOURCE: Polsby, Gallaher, and Rundquist (1969) and Stewart and Woon's Congressional
Committee Dataset.

The effect of the 1970s congressional reforms on committee chair selection quickly became evident. Figure 5.2 shows the increase in uncompensated seniority violations from the era of strong committee chairs up to the present. In 1975, the Democrats skipped over the most senior members of several committees and installed committee chairs who were more ideologically in tune with the party. Crook and Hibbing (1985) show that in the wake of the reforms and the seniority violations of 1975, sitting committee chairs as a group shifted ideologically to better reflect the mainstream of their party, presumably to avoid the same fate as the members who were skipped over in the 94th Congress. Notwithstanding these adjustments, occasional seniority violations were not uncommon through the 1980s and 1990s.

Recent Changes in Committee Chair Selection

When the Republicans took control of the House, incoming Speaker Newt Gingrich acted quickly on committee chair appointments before most new members of Congress had even come to Washington. By his swift action, Gingrich essentially asserted that the power to select committee chairs was his (Aldrich and Rohde 1997–98). While Gingrich followed the norm of seniority in most instances, seniority violations in selecting chairs for four committees (Agriculture, Appropriations, Energy and Commerce, and Judiciary) demonstrated that Republican leaders were willing to violate seniority to ensure that committee chairs were loyal to the party.

After the initial round of committee chair appointments had already taken place, the new Republican majority formalized rules for selecting committee chairs that dramatically altered the committee chair selection process. The reforms placed a three-term (six-year) limit on committee chairs. Additionally, party leaders insisted that seniority would be just one factor among several in determining who would be selected to serve as committee chair. Taking the Democrats' lead, Republicans pronounced that party unity would be an important factor in selecting committee chairs (though Republicans clearly escalated the expected level of unity beyond what the Democrats had previously required). These reforms gave party leaders latitude to appoint their preferred candidates to committee chair positions.

The new Republican Conference rules call for a two-stage process for selecting committee chairs. First, the Republican Steering Committee makes "recommendations" to the Republican Conference. The Steering Committee is composed of twenty-six members. The committee is dominated by party leaders and by selected committee leaders, but is complemented by ten members who represent a geographic area of the country (selected by the other Republican members in that area of the country), as well as by a representative for states with fewer than three Republican members (if there are no geographic representatives to the committee who are from a state with fewer than three Republican members). The committee is dominated by the Speaker, who gets five votes on matters before the committee. The majority leader has two votes, and all other members get one vote. The recommendations of the Steering Committee are passed on to the Republican Conference. While the Conference can vote individually on each committee chair recommendation, they sometimes approve the recommendations of the Steering Committee in one or more groups[2] (Schneider 2002, Deering and Wahlbeck 2006). Committee chairs for the 105th and 106th Congresses were selected by this process, with just a handful of violations occurring.

While Gingrich was the architect of these reforms, he did not remain in Congress long enough to oversee the implementation of the committee chair term limits. Following the 2000 elections, under the speakership of Dennis Hastert, the class of Republican committee chairs who began service in 1995 became the first cohort of committee chairs subjected to term limits. Hastert crafted a process, first used in the 107th Congress, where members wishing to serve as committee chairs applied for the positions and were interviewed by the full Steering Committee. However, it was not clear to members precisely what the criteria were for successfully winning a position. Republican Party rules stated that the chairs would not necessarily go to the most senior applicant. Did the leadership really mean that?

The results of the new application process from the 107th to 109th Congresses show that the leadership has no qualms about violating seniority. Indeed, a solid majority of committee chair races in these Congresses were won by members with less seniority than other applicants for the position. If seniority is no longer the factor that determines committee chairs, what has taken its place? Exchange theory predicts that if party leaders are free to violate seniority, they will use their powers to name these chairs to further party goals. Two of these prominent goals, discussed previously, center on securing a majority (which requires money) and the passage of policy (which requires unified voting of party voting, especially when a party has only a small majority). We now move to a discussion of competing theories of legislative organization to see what predictions each theory would make regarding seniority, member-to-member and member-to-party contributions, and party unity in voting.

Theories of Party Power and Congressional Organization

Congressional Organization and Seniority

Gilligan and Krehbiel (1987) and Krehbiel (1991) contend that the U.S. Congress is organized on an *informational* basis. Committees and all facets of the institution are assembled to maximize the spread of policy knowledge in the chamber and to increase its use. While informational theorists allow for some seniority violations, they contend that a norm of seniority is crucial in order to encourage members to specialize and to develop expertise in specific policy areas.

The informational perspective stands in contrast to the *distributive* view of Congress (Weingast and Marshall 1988). Proponents of the distributive organization hypothesis explain that members of Congress are concerned solely with their own reelection, so they make trades with other legislators on issues that are not relevant to their constituency so as to forge a coalition that can pass legislation that will help its members maximize their reelection opportunities. The distributive view is pork-barrel politics at its finest (or worst). Among the assumptions that are necessary to make such exchanges workable, according to Weingast and Marshall, is a committee system with the traditional seniority norm where members of Congress have a property right to a chair position by virtue of length of service and cannot be deprived of it.

Neither of these perspectives explicitly includes the influence of the party. Indeed, in a follow-up study, Krehbiel (1993) contends that under the conditions of an informatively organized legislature, parties would have little or no influence on congressional operations. Indeed, both the distributive and informational theories of legislative organization are compatible with a committee system where party leaders select committee chairs with little weight given to seniority. In contrast, a third perspective on legislative organization places parties as the driving force behind legislative organization (including the previously discussed party cartel and conditional party government schools of thought, e.g., Cox and McCubbins 1993, Aldrich 1995, Rohde 1991). Party cartel theorists would contend that the committee chair selection power always belongs to the majority party and does not hinge on the distribution of preferences among its members. In contrast, proponents of conditional party government would concede that the party will only possess the ability to select committee chairs when the majority party is internally homogeneous and ideologically distant from the minority. Given the substantial fluctuation in violations of seniority in Figures 5.1 and 5.2, it seems that conditional party government theory better explains party control of committee chairs. However, even if the power to select committee chairs is conditional, when parties have it, the exchange theory suggests that parties may offer these positions in exchange for the support of party goals.

Party Goals, Committee Chairs, and the Exchange Theory

The fundamental argument of the exchange theory of party influence claims that parties assist members of Congress in realizing their goals in exchange for those members working to advance the goals of the party. In the context of committee chair selection, the relevant goal of members of Congress is that of obtaining power in Washington (Fenno 1973). Exchange theory predicts that if parties could control the selection of committee chairs, they could offer those positions to help members achieve that goal in exchange for the support of party goals.

We have already discussed the two key goals of political parties, majority control and good policy (as defined by the party). To reach these goals, the party must maintain a majority in Congress. To this end, a significant arm of each party focuses on supporting the election and reelection of its candidates. The NRCC and the DCCC, for example, offer campaign support to candidates. Some of the support comes in the form of endorsements, advice on campaign strategy, and pre-fabricated campaign ads (Jacobson 2004). Parties also make significant amounts of direct contributions to candidates (Herrnson 2004). Since the 1996 Supreme Court ruling in *Colorado Republican Federal Campaign Committee v. FEC*, party committees have also been allowed to make independent expenditures on behalf of candidates. Complementing the support of party committees, party members with excess funds (especially those holding leadership positions) make contributions to the campaigns of members in need. It has become conventional wisdom that it takes a lot of money to win a congressional election. Similarly, in today's competitive political environment, it takes a massive amount of funding for a party to gain or maintain control of Congress.

Simply asking members for those funds seems to be problematic because individual members are not likely to part with their funds unless they have an incentive to do so. In chapter 2, we saw that incumbents who seek to further their ambitions seem to be the most active in raising funds for the party and for other candidates. Party leaders may offer committee chair positions as a selective incentive to encourage members of Congress to contribute funds to further the party's goal of gaining or maintaining majority status.

Still, money and a majority are not enough to reach the goals of a party. If the party seeks to enact its policy agenda, it needs a *cohesive* majority. In chapter 4, I showed that one way in which parties build cohesion is by providing funds to assist members in obtaining their electoral goals. However, if a political party can control committee chair appointments, party leaders could also use these valuable chair assignments as an incentive to cultivate voting loyalty among aspiring committee chairs.

Hypotheses and Data

Based on the exchange theory, this chapter seeks to test four key hypotheses. The hypothesis we must initially test regards the role of seniority in the committee chair selection process. In order for exchange theory to apply to committee chair selection, we must first show that seniority has been at least weakened to the point where party leaders can control the selection process. The traditional rule of seniority that characterized most Congresses in the twentieth century afforded the most senior member of a committee a veritable property right to chair their committee. Along these lines, Polsby, Gallaher, and Rundquist (1969, 790) contended that "like pregnancy, seniority is for most purposes a dichotomous variable." The seniority system points to one individual who should chair the committee, and if the individual with the greatest committee seniority does not chair that committee, seniority has been violated. One possible exception occurs when the most senior member accepts an assignment of greater value, such as a different committee chair position. Even in this situation, the next most senior contender for the position can be identified, and if that individual is not selected, seniority is violated. This perspective yields the following hypothesis:

> H_{1A}: *The Absolute Seniority Hypothesis:* The committee chair candidate with the longest period of continuous service on a committee will be selected as its chair.

A different perspective on seniority, however, may be in order. While the most senior member may not always be selected, parties may still consider length of service. That is, parties may not be willing to grant a first- or second-term member a committee chair position. This perspective departs from the traditional definition of "seniority" as being determinative of chair selection, but reflects the notion that experience on a committee may have some bearing on committee selection. This yields the Relative Seniority Hypothesis:

> H_{1B}: *The Relative Seniority Hypothesis:* The longer a committee chair candidate has continuously served on a committee, the greater the probability that he or she will be selected as its chair.

To test the *absolute seniority hypothesis*, I determined who the most senior candidate for a committee was by examining the committee roster in the Congress preceding the Congress when the appointment was made. The most senior candidate for each chair is coded as 1, with all other candidates coded zero. To test the *relative seniority hypothesis*, I code a variable as the number of Congresses in which a legislator has consecutively served on the committee they seek to chair.

In addition to a diminished role for seniority, the exchange theory implies that party leaders will offer committee chair positions as an incentive for members to fundraise in support of party goals and to vote in support of the party's preferred positions. As outlined earlier, members of Congress may make contributions to party committees and to fellow party members from their personal campaign funds (PCCs) and/or through a leadership PAC. When a committee chair becomes vacant, party leaders may consider the ability of each chair-aspirant to raise funds for the party. If so, committee chair races may become veritable fund-raising contests to see who can contribute the most money to party candidates and to party committees. Are members effectively able to "buy" assignments from the party by making large contributions in support of party committees and same-party candidates? This question motivates our second hypothesis.

H_2: *The Fundraising Capacity Hypothesis:* Candidates who contribute more funds to support party goals will be more likely to win committee chair contests.

To test the fundraising capacity hypothesis, I sum the total amount of *contributions* each candidate made to their party's committees and fellow-party candidates. These contributions come from both PCCs and from leadership PACs. Higher levels of contributions should result in winning a chair position.

In a recent paper examining committee chair selection, Deering and Wahlbeck (2006) propose examining separate effects for leadership PAC contributions to candidates, contributions from a representative's personal campaign committee to other candidates, and contributions from candidates to the NRCC (but not leadership PAC contributions to the NRCC). These distinctions are not theoretically well-supported by the literature on member-to-member and member-to-party contributions (Wilcox 1989; Heberlig 2003; Kuhn 1999; Heberlig and Larson 2005; Heberlig, Hetherington, and Larson 2006) which argue that all of these types of contributions are manifestations of party support (Deering and Wahlbeck suggest that contributions from a leadership PAC are an indicator of dissent because the money goes directly to candidates rather than being filtered through the NRCC). Further, the results in the Deering and Wahlbeck paper are somewhat inconsistent with their specified expectations for each type of contribution. As such, I proceed to evaluate candidate financial support of the party and party candidates as a single variable.[3]

Next, party leaders not only want to have proficient fund-raisers as committee chairs, but they also want chairs who will support the policy goals of the party. Thus, members must establish a record of party support if they hope to secure a committee chair position. During the era of strong committee chairs, discord plagued the Democratic Party in part because some committee chairs (particularly conservative southern Democrats) were unwilling to support positions that were supported by a majority of their own party. To avoid this problem, today's Republican leaders may only be willing to appoint a committee chair who will support party positions.

H_3: *The Party Support Hypothesis:* Candidates who consistently support party positions will be more likely to win committee chair contests.

CQ *party unity* scores for each committee chair candidate are used to test the party support hypothesis. These scores indicate the percentage of the time that a member of Congress votes with a majority of his or her party when a majority of one party votes against a majority of the other party. The scores show whether a member has demonstrated ideological support for party positions. While this measure may have some limitations (see Krehbiel 2000), journalistic accounts of committee chair interviews reveal that committee chair aspirants brag about high CQ party unity scores to provide evidence to the Steering Committee that they regularly support party positions. When members of Congress want to know whether or not a member supports the party, they generally reference these scores. Because gavels will be awarded on the *perception* of unity rather than on the actual level of unity, we can more accurately test the party support hypothesis using party unity scores that actually reflect the perceptions of the Steering Committee.[4]

Finally, party leaders may prefer to place electorally safe members of Congress in committee chair positions. *Electoral safety* is measured using the percentage of the two-party vote each committee chair aspirant received in the election prior to their chair candidacy.

H_4: *Electoral Safety Hypothesis:* Candidates who win election with a higher percentage of the two-party vote share are more likely to win a committee chair position.

These hypotheses will be tested on data from the three different regimes of chair selection during Republican rule in the House of Representatives. In the 104th Congress, incoming speaker Newt Gingrich simply asserted the power to name the committee chairs and a slate was prepared before most freshmen representatives had even come to Washington (Aldrich and Rohde 1997–1998). A second regime of committee chair selection prevailed in the 105th and 106th Congresses where the Steering Committee led the selection process but did not use an interview process and term limits had not yet taken effect. A final regime of committee chair selection developed beginning in the 107th Congress and persisted through the end of Republican control of the House in the 109th Congress. In this regime, term limits forced sitting chairs to relinquish their gavels after six years and new chairs were chosen by the Steering Committee using Hastert's interview process. Table 5.1 lists the committees with contested races in the period under study. In Table 5.2, the reader will find summary statistics for each of the relevant variables in each time period.

TABLE 5.1 Contested Committee Chair Races, 104th–109th Congresses

104th	105th	106th	107th	108th	109th
Agriculture	Agriculture	Agriculture	Armed Services	Agriculture	Appropriations
Appropriations	Government Reform	Appropriations	Banking	Government Reform	Veterans Affairs
Armed Services		Rules	Budget		
	Science			Resources	
Banking			Education		
	Small Business				
Budget			Energy and Commerce		
Education			Financial Services		
Energy and Commerce			International Relations		
Government Reform			Judiciary		
House Administration			Small Business		
International Relations			Veterans Affairs		
Intelligence			Ways and Means		
Judiciary					
Resources					
Rules					
Science					
Small Business					
Transportation					
Veterans Affairs					
Ways and Means					

TABLE 5.2 Summary Statistics

		Mean	Std. Dev.	Min.	Max.
Contributions	104th	$16,749	44,128	0	463,153
	105–106th	$36,911	69,657	0	669,773
	107–109th	$236,152	53,295	1,000	1,790,000
Seniority (Terms)	104th	3.08	2.95	1	15
	105–106th	2.38	2.17	0*	13
	107–109th	7.39	3.52	0**	14
Party Unity	104th	88.83	7.47	59	98
	105–106th	87.89	8.56	48	97.5
	107–109th	89.80	7.31	71.5	98
Electoral Safety	104th	73.18%	73.18	50	100
(Previous Vote %)	105–106th	66.37%	14.01	46	100
	107–109th	67.27%	9.62	50	100

*Robert F. Smith had retired after the 103rd Congress but returned in the 105th Congress. Seniority rules count *continuous* service, so while Smith is identified as a candidate for the Agriculture Committee chair in the 105th Congress, his number of terms of seniority is 0.

**Christopher Cox sought the Government Reform Committee chair in the 108th Congress even though he had not previously served on the committee.

SOURCE: Federal Election Commission, *CQ Weekly Report*, and Stewart and Woon's Congressional Committee Dataset.

Statistical Analysis

Approach

In a criticism of existing models of committee chair selection Cann (2006) outlines a number of methodological challenges in studying committee chair selection. Previous attempts to study committee chair selection have simply pooled all candidates for all committee chairs and modeled the probability of each member of Congress winning a chair position (Deering and Wahlbeck 2006). However, this method is substantively problematic in that it ignores the fact that members are engaged in races against specific candidates for specific chair positions. The approach is analogous to pooling every presidential candidate who ran in a general election between 1952 and 2004 in a single model and estimating the probability of each candidate winning. Such a model could end up predicting that Nixon and Kennedy were both elected in 1960, and that neither Clinton, Bush, nor Perot won in 1992. This substantive modeling failure results in a number of statistical problems—the observations are not independent, and the predicted probabilities for all candidates for a chair position are not constrained to sum to 1. Further, there is no guarantee that the number of predicted chair winners (using the naive $p > .5$ criterion) will be equal to the number of open chair positions. Cann shows that these problems result in inconsistent estimates in the Deering and Wahlbeck model.

Rather than pooling all observations, I apply a method developed in economics for studying qualitative choice behavior. The conditional logit model (McFadden 1974) is appropriate for determining the influence of independent variables on the choice of a particular option from choices within a particular choice set. The size of the choice set, as well as the options within the choice set, need not be the same across all choice sets. Thus, the model is perfect for analyzing the determinants of chair selection where there are different numbers of candidates seeking different chair positions. The major advantage of this model is that rather than considering the level of fund-raising (or unity, seniority, or electoral safety) relative to all chair candidates, the conditional logit model analyzes a chair candidate's level of fund-raising (or unity, seniority, or electoral safety) *relative only to the candidates he or she is running against.* In other words, $300,000 of fund-raising may be enough to win a chair position if your opponent raised only $100,000. However, if you face an opponent who raised $1 million, $300,000 will almost certainly not be enough.

A further statistical complication comes because we observe the entire population of committee chair selection in each era rather than being able to make repeated draws from an infinite population (an assumption required for classical statistics in order to create a margin of error). This problem is remedied by the application of a Bayesian estimator for the conditional logit model as discussed in Cann (2006). The statistical appendix to this chapter offers a basic explanation of the larger issues, but the reader is referred to Cann for a more technical treatment.

Finally, the Deering and Wahlbeck (2006) effort only considers chair selection in the 107th Congress. To show the transition from a system based on seniority to a system based on money and party unity, I analyze committee chair selection from the 104th Congress (the system where Gingrich asserted the power to select all committee chairs), then turn to committee chair selection from the 105th to 106th Congresses (where the Steering Committee made choices without interviews and before term limits had taken effect), and finally consider the current system (107th–109th Congresses where term limits forced sitting chairs from office and the Steering Committee interviewed committee chair applicants). To test both the absolute and relative seniority hypotheses, I run the model twice for each period, once using a dummy indicating the most senior member among the applicants and once using the number of terms served on the committee.

Committee Chair Selection in the 104th Congress

With Republicans taking control of the House in the 104th Congress all committee chairs needed to be filled. For the purposes of this analysis, all Republicans who had served on a given committee in the 103rd Congress and did not have another leadership position were considered as possible chairs for that committee. The conditional logit model results are estimated using standard Bayesian estimation techniques.[5] The results of the analysis are presented in Table 5.3.

Accounts of committee chair selection in this period note that while Gingrich did violate seniority in a handful of instances, most of the time he made decisions on the basis of seniority (Aldrich and Rohde 1997–98, Brewer and Deering 2005). The statistical results support this conclusion, showing that seniority was the key determinant of committee chair selection. In this period, financial support of the party and party unity had no significant effect on committee chair selection. Electoral safety similarly appears to have little influence on the outcomes of these races.

TABLE 5.3 Bayesian Conditional Logit Model of Committee Chair Selection for the 104th Congress

	Absolute Seniority Model	Relative Seniority Model
Seniority	3.767**	.704**
	(2.697, 4.829)	(.433, .995)
Contributions (in thousands)	−.006	−.005
	(−.026, .012)	(−.025, .010)
Party Unity	.019	.043
	(−.075, .118)	(−.058, .147)
Electoral Safety	-.028	−.014
	(−.080, .023)	(−.061, .031)
Percent Correctly Predicted[6]	83.3%	72.2%
n	259	259
Model DIC[7]	37.876	50.524

Bayesian Conditional Logit analysis of Committee Chair Selection. Coefficient estimates are posterior means, with 95% Highest Posterior Densities in parentheses.

**Denotes posteriors that do not contain zero in the 95% HPD interval.

SOURCE: Federal Election Commission, Stewart and Woon's Congressional Committee Dataset, and various issues of *CQ Weekly Report*.

In some sense, the general statistical result may not accurately portray Gingrich's lack of enthusiasm for the seniority system. Some have noted that while Gingrich didn't immediately eliminate the seniority system, he did choose his violations carefully—while he didn't violate seniority on every committee, he violated seniority for the most critical positions (especially the Appropriations Committee) and waited to see how the other appointees would behave (Aldrich and Rohde 1997–98).

Committee Chair Selection in the 105th–106th Congresses

Committee chair selection in the 105th and 106th Congresses has been characterized as the proverbial "calm before the storm." Treatments of committee chair selection in these Congresses again suggest that seniority remained the key to winning a chair position (Renka and Ponder 2005). We consider here the races to fill vacant chair positions in the 105th and 106th Congresses. As in the analysis of the 104th Congress, all individuals who had served on a committee in the previous Congress are considered candidates for the chair position in the following Congress. The statistical results for this period appear in Table 5.4.[8]

TABLE 5.4 Bayesian Conditional Logit Model of Committee Chair Selection for the 105th–106th Congresses

	Absolute Seniority Model	Relative Seniority Model
Seniority	3.089**	.824**
	(.808, 5.489)	(.287, 1.437)
Contributions (in thousands)	.016	.022**
	(−.003, .039)	(.0001, 1.437)
Party Unity	-.041	.029
	(−.151, .079)	(−.098, .167)
Electoral Safety	.025	.009
	(−.064, .108)	(−.084, .096)
Percent Correctly Predicted	57%	71%
n	141	141
Model DIC	32.910	29.410

Bayesian Conditional Logit analysis of Committee Chair Selection. Coefficient estimates are posterior means, with 95% Highest Posterior Densities in parentheses.

**Denotes posteriors that do not contain zero in the 95% HPD interval.

SOURCE: Federal Election Commission, Stewart and Woon's Congressional Committee Dataset, and various issues of *CQ Weekly Report*.

The results strongly support the continued importance of seniority in this period. For example, the model predicts that the most senior member of the Science Committee, James Sensenbrenner, will win the chair position. However, if the next most senior member, Sherwood Boehlert, had served even just one term longer than Sensenbrenner, both the absolute and relative seniority models would predict Boehlert as the winner instead. However, it also shows that financial support of party goals became a significant predictor of committee chair selection in this period (at least in the relative seniority model). If Boehlert had contributed about $30,000 more (for a total of $73,250), his probability of winning would have been greater than Sensenberenner (who contributed no money at all).

Committee Chair Selection in the 107th–109th Congresses

The 107th Congress was the first Congress where sitting committee chairs were removed from their positions under the term limits established by House Republicans. It also introduced the interview process that allows us to identify specifically which members of Congress were under consideration for each chair position. As such, rather than using all members of each committee as potential chairs, in this section we consider only those who interviewed for committee chairs as possible winners. Deering and Wahlbeck (2006) concluded that seniority had been weakened and that financial support of the party and party unity had become important factors in addition to seniority in the 107th Congress. However, the methodological problems discussed previously show that they have inaccurately quantified the determinants chair selection in the 107th Congress. Further, chair selection in the 108th and 109th Congresses has not been rigorously studied. As such, a re-analysis of the 107th–109th Congresses is essential to understanding the true effects of seniority, fund-raising, and party unity. The statistical results for this period appear in Table 5.5.[9]

These results reveal a very different dynamic than was present in the 104th–106th Congresses. Perhaps the most remarkable result from the model is that seniority has no influence on the outcome of each committee chair contest in these two Congresses. The results from the absolute seniority model show that the traditional seniority system where the most senior member of a committee has an automatic right to a chair has been effectively dismantled. Further, even when we consider the possible influence of the *relative* level of seniority (measured in terms of continuous service), we find that seniority has no significant effect on committee chair selection in the 107th–109th Congresses.

Equally remarkable are the findings for the influence of financial support and party unity. The level of contributions to party committees and to fellow-party candidates is a strong, significant predictor of success in securing a committee chair. Furthermore, the coefficient on party unity is at least marginally significant, with the 90 percent highest posterior density interval not containing 0.[10] The results show that in making committee chair appointments in the

TABLE 5.5 Bayesian Conditional Logit Model of Committee Chair Selection for the 107th–109th Congresses

	Absolute Seniority Model	Relative Seniority Model
Seniority	.779	−.031
	(−.750, 2.348)	(−.552, .481)
Contributions	.016**	.017**
(in thousands)	(.003, .029)	(.003, .033)
Party Unity	.163*	.160*
	(−.014, .367)	(−.0126, .356)
Electoral Safety	.011	.009
	(−.137, .163)	(−.131, .158)
Percent Correctly Predicted	80.0%	80.0%
n	43	43
Model DIC	23.922	24.843

Bayesian Conditional Logit analysis of Committee Chair Selection. Coefficient estimates are posterior means, with 95% Highest Posterior Densities in parentheses.

*Denotes posteriors that do not contain zero in the 90% HPD interval.

**indicates that 0 is not in the 95% HPD interval.

SOURCE: Federal Election Commission, Stewart and Woon's Congressional Committee Dataset, and various issues of *CQ Weekly Report*.

107th through 109th Congresses, the Republican Steering Committee departed from the classic seniority system to a system where committee appointments are made to advance party goals.

Overall, the results show that in making committee chair appointments in the 107th through 109th Congresses, the Republican Steering Committee successfully moved away from the seniority system to a system where committee appointments are made to advance party goals. To facilitate a more thorough interpretation of the model, I present predicted probabilities that summarize the effects of seniority, fund-raising, and party unity.

Four candidates sought the International Relations chair in 2000 when the term limits rule created a vacancy. Jim Leach (R-IA) had served ten terms on the committee and was next in line by seniority. However, Leach is among the most liberal Republican members of the House. Further, Leach did little in the way of fund-raising on behalf of the party or its candidates, donating only $5,000.

Notwithstanding Leach's unimpressive support of party goals, by the standard of the traditional seniority system, the chair would have been Leach's.

Leach's chief competitor, Henry Hyde (R-IL), had chaired the Judiciary Committee for six years, but the term limits rule compelled him to step down. When Hyde saw that the term limits would indeed be enforced, he threw his hat into the ring for the International Relations Committee. In contrast to Leach, Hyde showed support of party goals with a party unity score near 90 and more than $100,000 in contributions to the Republican Party and to Republican candidates. Two other candidates also entered the race, Douglas Bereuter of Nebraska and Chris Smith of New Jersey, whose fund-raising and unity scores were better than Leach's, but not as strong as Hyde's.

The black line in Figure 5.3 shows the predicted probabilities of Hyde winning the race while varying his spending, and holding all other variables constant at their observed values (for all candidates).[11] Because Hyde's party unity score was so much higher than the other candidates, he would have narrowly been the predicted winner of the race even if he had not contributed money to the party or to party candidates. However, higher levels of contributions make it much more likely that Hyde would win the chair. The model also shows that more aggressive fund-raising could have snatched the race for another candidate. The darker and lighter gray lines and the dashed line reflect the probabilities of Bereuter, Smith, and Leach, respectively, winning the race while varying their spending and holding all other variables constant at their their observed values. If Bereuter had donated just over $180,000 (about $70,000 more than Hyde) he would have become the most likely winner of the

FIGURE 5.3 Predicted Probabilities for Winning the International Relations Committee Chair

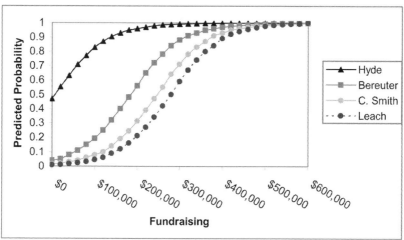

race as predicted by the model. Because Leach's party unity score was so low, victory for him would have been quite difficult, requiring him to raise nearly $300,000 to become the most likely winner of the race. This illustrates an important point—if a member of Congress has an extremely low loyalty score, it becomes very difficult (even nearly impossible in some cases) for that person to win a committee chair even with fairly strong fund-raising efforts.

A Qualitative Approach to Committee Chair Selection in the 107th–109th Congresses

An alternative approach to evaluating these hypotheses is to simply qualitatively consider the data. Given the relatively small number of candidates and races involved in the selection regime that has been in operation since the 107th Congress, we can simply examine the levels of fund-raising, seniority, and party unity to evaluate the relative importance in a non-technical, easy-to-understand way. Table 5.6 shows each committee chair candidate running for office and their respective levels of seniority, party unity, and fund-raising.

Only in 6 out of the 15 contested races did the candidate with the most seniority win the chair position.[12] In contrast, 11 of the 15 races went to the candidate who contributed the most money. Additionally, 9 of the 15 successful chair candidates had an average party unity score that was the highest (or

TABLE 5.6 Committee Chair Candidates, 107th–109th Congresses

	Committee	Party Name	Party Unity	Terms of Service	Contributions
107th Congress	Armed Services	Weldon	84.5	7	$157,200
		Hunter	92.5	10	$62,827
		Stump	*97*	*12*	*$197,520*
	Banking and	*Roukema*	*78.5*	*10*	*$40,000*
	Financial	Baker	92	6	$192,000
	Services	**Oxley**	**92.5**	**9[a]**	**$461,300**
	Budget	Smith, N.	91.5	4	$20,039
		Chambliss	*94.5*	*1[b]*	*$82,000*
		Sununu	95	2	$16,000
		Nussle	**90**	**3**	**$167,500**
	Energy and	Oxley	92.5	9	$461,300
	Commerce	*Tauzin*	*92.5*	*3[b]*	*$587,515*
	Education and	*Petri*	*87.5*	*11*	*$1,000*
	the Workforce	Hoekstra	93	4	$51,150
		Boehner	**94**	**1**	**$562,240**

(continued)

TABLE 5.6 (*continued*)

	Committee	Name	Party Unity	Terms of Service	Contributions
107th Congress	International Relations	Bereuter	80.5	9	$61,000
		Leach	*71.5*	*10*	*$5,000*
		Smith, C.	74.5	8	$53,000
		Hyde	**89**	**10**	**$107,100**
	Judiciary	Gekas	91.5	9	$47,000
		Sensenbrenner	*93*	*11*	*$134,000*
	Small Business	Kelly	72	3	$69,000
		Manzullo	*93.5*	*4*	*$32,300*
	Ways and Means	Shaw	86.5	7	$127,000
		Crane	*95*	*13*	*$348,196*
		Thomas	**90.5**	**9**	**$478,500**
	Veterans Affairs	Bilirakis	90.5	10	$107,750
		Smith, C.	*74.5*	*11*	*$53,000*
108th Congress	Agriculture	Smith, N.	91	7	$36,500
		Everett	98	7	$2,000
		Goodlatte	*98*	*7*	*$101,000*
	Government Reform	Cox	95.5	0	$383,400
		Shays	*77.5*	*8*	*$61,000*
		Davis, T.	**90**	**4**	**$568,700**
	Natural Resources	Duncan	91	6	$59,400
		Gallegly	*95*	*8*	*$63,098*
		Calvert	97	5	$115,500
		Pombo	**96**	**5**	**$25,000**
109th Congress	Appropriations	Rogers	96.5	10	$1,090,000
		Regula	*94*	*14*	*$1,037,000*
		Lewis	**94.5**	**11**	**$1,790,000**
	Veterans Affairs	**Buyer**	**96.5**	**7**	**$63,510**
		Smith, C.	*81*	*13*	*$76,000*

NOTES: Winning candidates are listed in **bold** type. The highest, ranking candidate is in *italics*. The list includes all contested committee chair races for the 107th–109th Congresses.

a. Oxley had served on the Commerce Committee in the 106th Congress. Part of that committee's jurisdiction was transferred to the Banking and Financial Services committee where Oxley was given a chair. Republican rules allowed Oxley to transfer his seniority on Energy and Commerce to the Banking and Financial Services Committee because of the jurisdictional change. Still, he was not the most senior candidate for that chair position.

b. These candidates had fewer actual terms of service than other candidates for the same committees but ranked higher on the committee roster in the preceding Congress, making them the most senior candidates.

SOURCES: Michael Malbin, Federal Elections Commission, Stewart and Woon's Congressional Committee Dataset, and *CQ Almanac*.

tied for the highest) among their competitors. The notion that fund-raising and unity now dominate the seniority norm as criteria for committee chair selection is further bolstered by the fact that of the 5 successful candidates who were the most senior among their respective fields, 3 were also the best fund-raisers among their competitors and 4 had the highest party unity score among their competitors. In other words, of the 5 successful senior members, the success of 4 can be attributed to their party unity scores and fund-raising activities rather than to their seniority. Only in the case of Chris Smith (chosen as chair of Veteran's Affairs) do we find Republican leaders choosing someone with more seniority over another candidate who had a better party unity score and made larger contributions.

Discussion

The major finding of this chapter is that House Republicans successfully secured the power to name committee chairs and that they select chairs in a manner consistent with the exchange theory of party influence. Both quantitative and qualitative methods show that in the 107th–109th Congresses (and to a lesser extent in the 105th–106th Congresses), committee chair candidates who help advance party goals through fund-raising are more likely to win the appointments they seek, regardless of their level of seniority. After taking control of Congress, House Republicans continued to abide by the seniority rule for a time, but have transitioned to a system that instead emphasizes support of the party both with voting and with financial support. The model at hand suggests that neither of these factors alone is sufficient to guarantee a committee chair position. Rather, candidates must reach an acceptable level of party unity before they can "buy" a committee chair. Similarly, candidates must contribute a certain amount of money before they can expect their record of party unity to carry them through.

In the case of the less-strict relative seniority model seniority, we could be witnessing a selection effect. It may be that only those who attain a certain level of seniority seek a committee chair position. Indeed, a *t*-test for difference of means shows that the group of candidates for committee chair positions has a significantly higher average level of committee seniority than the chamber as a whole.[13] Members of Congress must reach some level of seniority before they mount a campaign for a committee chair position. Still, once the field of candidates has been selected, seniority has no effect on the probability that a chair candidate wins the position he or she seeks.

Even with the possible selection effect, these results are still meaningful on two levels. First, the absolute seniority model is unaffected by the selection problem. The results from that model show that Republican leaders have simply abandoned the absolute seniority as the key criteria for committee chair selection. The classic system for committee chair selection that evolved after the revolt against Cannon has been replaced by a system where party support (demonstrated by voting records and financial contributions) determines committee chair selection.

Second, selection into the candidate pool by relative seniority would be most important if party leaders were forced to choose a chair from a pool of relatively high seniority members who did not meet their criteria for party support. However, from the pool of applicants, the party is nearly always able to find someone with an acceptable level of seniority who is also a loyal partisan and a financial supporter. It is rare to see someone appointed as chair when they have served on a committee for a short period of time. However, at the stage of final selection, it is those who make contributions and have strong voting records who are chosen to chair committees.[14]

The 110th Congress and Committee Chair Selection

The evidence presented here shows that the Republican Party has successfully altered the committee chair process to better serve party goals. The question remains unanswered regarding whether the new Democratic majority will follow the path of the Republicans. Historically, Democrats have shown some willingness to make an example of a few disloyal senior committee members to encourage loyalty among their committee chairs (Crook and Hibbing 1985), but they have nevertheless largely kept the seniority norm in tact. While we have only a single Congress to consider, there are a number of indicators that Democrats will not use seniority as the sole criterion for selecting committee chairs.

First, incoming speaker Nancy Pelosi (D-CA) surprised her caucus by announcing that she would retain the six-year term limits on committee chairs developed by Republicans. Barney Frank (D-MA), a staunch Pelosi supporter, justified the choice, saying, "I think we suffered the last time the Democrats were in power from too much chairman autonomy," and then added, "Accusing the speaker of trying to manage public policy is like accusing the fire department of trying to fight fire" (Weisman 2007). While Frank, a committee chair himself, is supportive, the remaining committee chairs were rather resistant to the notion that they would be forced from their positions in six years. Citing an unnamed Democratic source, *The Hill* reported that incoming Appropriations Committee chair David Obey (D-WI) refused to come to the floor to cast his vote for Pelosi as Speaker of the House until he was advised that Pelosi would give later consideration to granting exceptions to the term limits (Kaplan 2007).[15] Second, Pelosi exercised her authority to skip over Jane Harman (D-CA) (and others) to appoint Silvestre Reyes (D-TX) as chair of the House Select Committee on Intelligence. While the rationale for the seniority violations involves personal clashes between Harman and Pelosi, the violation sends a message that seniority is not inviolable in a Democratic Congress.

Taken together, these two indicators suggest that while House Democrats have kept seniority violations to a minimum, they have sent a clear message to their committee chairs that they are expected to support party goals or they risk losing their positions. If the most senior members of each committee support the goals of the party, they are upholding their responsibilities in the exchange of "power in Washington" for "support of party goals," making it appear that seniority is in operation when it is only being propped up by actions consistent with the exchange theory of party influence. The Democrats stand now in a position similar to where Republicans stood in 1994—seniority is still an important factor, but the message is written on the wall that members of Congress can no longer view seniority as a sure bet for winning a committee chair position. More time is needed to ascertain the degree to which member contributions, party unity, and seniority will be weighed in selecting committee chairs in Democratic-controlled Congresses.

Implications for Theories of Congressional Organization

These findings have important ramifications for partisan theories of congressional organization. Of the three leading theories (partisan, informational, and distributive), these findings lend support only to partisan theories of legislative organization (the conditional party government, party cartel, and exchange theories). Seniority is a pillar of distributive theory. The move away from seniority makes it impossible for average legislators to obtain the distributive powers associated with a committee chair position. Instead, the new system bestows the distributive powers of committee chairs on party loyalists who can work against logrolls that do not favor the majority party. In part, this ensures that the distributive power of committee chairs is kept under the tight rein of party loyalists. However, it also bestows the benefits that come with being a committee chair (i.e., distributive power) exclusively on party loyalists.

From the standpoint of informational theory, seniority is critically important. Krehbiel (1991) argues that the practice of seniority is important because it provides an incentive for members to specialize. While occasional violations of seniority are not wholly incompatible with this perspective, the persistent violations that have marked the 107th–109th Congresses are not. Further, the criteria that have replaced the seniority norm are not compatible with the notion of informational organization in Congress. Placing party loyalists in committee chair positions is clearly incompatible with the fundamental tenets of informational theory, and it is difficult to imagine an informationally organized legislature auctioning chair positions for its committees.

In contrast the results in this chapter provide strong evidence that Congress increasingly operates on the basis of partisan operation. Only partisan theories of party governance would allow for a majority party being given the power to hand-pick loyalists and strong fund-raisers for positions of power in the legislature at the cost of seniority. However, the results can be shown to be more supportive of some variants of partisan theories of congressional organization than others.

The Exchange Theory and Other Theories of Party Influence

We have shown that the majority party is willing to provide the benefits of a committee chair position to loyalists (who will use the power of the chair in accordance with the wishes of party leadership) and individuals who offer the financial support the party needs to maintain a majority. Such arrangements dovetail with the propositions of the exchange theory: Committee chair candidates who most distinguish themselves from their competition in terms of support for party goals are rewarded with the chair position they seek.

These results also dovetail with the predictions of conditional party government theory. The marked homogeneity of the Republican Party in the 1995–2006 period led to a substantial weakening of the seniority system, and to the placement of demonstrated party loyalists in positions of authority. The temporal sway in the importance of seniority is more easily explained by conditional party government theory because it is consistent with changes in the homogeneity of the majority party. Explaining the changes in the effects of seniority over time poses greater problems for the party cartel theory, which predicts more stability in the powers of the majority party. While Cox and McCubbins (1993) note that there has never been a committee chair selected who is not from the majority party, it is clear that the type of majority party member selected as a chair in the 1960s (or even the 1990s) is different from the people selected for these positions in times where parties are more ideologically cohesive (e.g., the 107th–109th Congresses or the Cannon era).

While the evidence at hand is compelling, it leaves several questions unanswered. Given the retention of committee chair term limits, it is premature to draw conclusions on the importance of fund-raising and party unity for committee chair selection in a Democratic House. In addition, the conditional party government theory predicts that this arrangement will only be able to endure as long as the majority party remains quite homogeneous. Given the historical fluctuations in the distribution of preferences in the House, it seems likely that seniority will, at some point, make a resurgence. Nevertheless, this chapter shows that where party leaders are able to control the committee chair selection process, they use that power in a manner consistent with exchange theory.

Statistical Appendix

McFadden's (1974) choice model estimates the probability of choosing choice *j* from choice set *i*, as in:

$$p\,(y_{ij} = 1) = \frac{\exp(x'_{ij}\,\beta)}{\sum_{j=1}^{J}\exp\,(x'_{ij}\,\beta)}$$

where the probability of making choice *j* depends on several variables, contained in *x*, with β being a vector of coefficients relating the variables to the probability of being selected. This setup constrains the probabilities of winning a specific chair position for all candidates to equal 1.

McFadden (1974) proposes an estimation of this model via maximum likelihood (ML) methods. Cann (2006) discusses a Bayesian estimator of the conditional logit model and argues that it is superior on the grounds of flexibility with small sample sizes and no required assumptions about repeated sampling from an infinite population—both potential problems for ML estimation of the conditional logit model in committee chair contest data.

CHAPTER 6

Member Contributions and Control of the House Appropriations Committee

When the founders drafted the Constitution, they felt that Congress would most likely be the most powerful branch of the new government because it held the power of the purse. While the relative strength of the legislative, judicial, and executive branches have fluctuated over time, it is clear that the power of the purse has made the House Appropriations Committee a powerful force in the American political system. In chapter 5, we saw that party leaders may use committee chair positions as incentives to encourage members to support the collective goals of their respective parties. The importance of the Appropriations Committee chair position was highlighted in Table 5.6 where we saw that the three Appropriations Committee chair candidates in the 109th Congress together contributed nearly $4 million to the party and to party committees.

The congressional reforms of the 1970s substantially strengthened the powers of subcommittee chairs (Rohde 1991). The subcommittee chairs on the House Appropriations Committee are certainly no exception—Because of the substantial powers that come with controlling spending, the thirteen subcommittee chairs on the committee have been dubbed the "Cardinals of Capitol Hill" (Munson 1993). Subcommittee chairs on Appropriations are widely held to be equal in power to the full committee chairs of other committees. It seems possible, then, that if congressional leaders could control the selection of the Appropriations subcommittee chairs, this would provide an additional bargaining chip to exchange with rank-and-file members of Congress in order to encourage support of party goals. It is natural to ask who in Congress gets to hold these positions, and whether the selection criteria are consistent with the exchange theory.

House Republican Conference Rules allow the chair of a full committee to name a slate of subcommittee chairs based on whatever criteria he or she chooses (though a majority of Republican members on the full committee can "disapprove" of the process established by the committee chair). Beginning in the 108th Congress, Speaker Dennis Hastert and Majority Leader Tom DeLay pushed through a rules change requiring Appropriations subcommittee chairs to win the approval of the Steering Committee in a process much like that required for full committee chairs described in chapter 5. As with full committee chairs, Republican leaders have emphasized that the selection of these subcommittee chairs should not be based on seniority alone (Schneider 2004).

Willis (2002) cites remarks by members of Congress to illustrate the importance of two factors aside from seniority. First, Republicans seek to appoint members of Congress who will advance policies of fiscal restraint as advocated by the party. Second, and of interest to the primary topic of this book, party members expect Appropriations subcommittee chairs to raise substantial amounts of money through their PCCs and leadership PACs and then to contribute those funds to the party and to party candidates. In short, many party members count on the party for fund-raising assistance, and they expect party leaders to provide incentives to get members who have more resources, to share their resources with other members and with the party. One of these incentives could be a position as a subcommittee chair on the House Appropriations Committee. In this chapter, I analyze the determinants of Appropriations subcommittee chair selection to assess the extent to which party leaders are able to offer leadership positions on the Appropriations Committee to members in exchange for support of party goals (particularly party unity and fund-raising).

Political Parties and the Power of the Cardinals

Aldrich and Rohde (2000) show that while the powers of the Appropriations subcommittee chairs are quite substantial, throughout most of the twentieth century the powers vested in the cardinals have not been used to advance party goals. Fenno (1966) notes that the work of the Appropriations subcommittees has historically been deliberative and organized around seniority norms. Subcommittees were expected to adhere to a norm of minimal partisanship. Fenno's (1973) treatment of committees found the Appropriations Committee to be both very decentralized (placing a great deal of power in the hands of subcommittee chairs) and the least partisan of the committees he studied. White's (1989) study of the Appropriations Committee finds that while parties do strive to place party loyalists on the committee, they also seek "responsible" members who seem to conform more or less to the norms of the committee that continued to be relatively decentralized and nonpartisan.

When Republicans took control of the House after the 1994 elections, they found that they had a relatively homogeneous group of legislators who were willing to consolidate power in a stronger speaker (Aldrich and Rohde 1997–98). Notwithstanding a multitude of committee reforms, many Republicans (including the leadership) thought that the committee system would still not be a safe mechanism for advancing the interests of the new majority. In particular, Aldrich and Rohde (2000) noted that senior Republicans may have had loyalties to their committees that were as strong (or stronger) than their loyalties to the party. Rather than controlling the legislative output of the entire committee system, the solution was to control the appropriations process by increasing partisan control over the Appropriations Committee. The risk that Republican leaders incurred in pursuing this strategy concerned the difficulty of overcoming deeply embedded norms of decentralization and nonpartisanship in the Appropriations subcommittees.

The theory of conditional party government holds that when the majority party is internally homogeneous and externally polarized, its members will grant more power to the leadership. Aldrich and Rohde (2000) provide ample evidence that in the Republican era the conditions of conditional party government have been met. If the ebb and flow of party strength gave the Republican Party the power to influence the selection of subcommittee chair selection, the exchange theory predicts that party leaders would use these positions in exchanges with party members to encourage support of party goals in spite of the norms of the Appropriations Committee. This would enable Republican leadership to reach the party's policy goals by controlling the allocation of governmental funds while avoiding the perils of the committee system.

Controlling the Cardinals

Aldrich and Rohde compile impressive evidence that the Republicans were effective at using their powers to get desired outcomes generally (1997–98) and specifically through the Appropriations Committee (2000), particularly focusing on the early years of the Republican era. Nevertheless, their work generally focuses on legislative techniques (e.g., agenda control techniques, restrictive rules, and floor amendments) rather than on the recruitment of members to the committee.[1] While they do devote time to discussing leadership efforts to persuade sitting committee and subcommittee leaders (as well as rank-and-file committee members), they spend less time on leadership efforts to control who occupies those positions.[2]

Almost immediately after the results of the 1994 elections were clear, Newt Gingrich asserted the authority to name the committee chairs for the 104th Congress. While the results in chapter 5 suggest that demonstrating party loyalty through fund-raising and voting unity did not become the key factors (rather than seniority) in winning a committee chair position until the 107th Congress, given the prominence and power of the Appropriations Committee, Gingrich was sure to name a stalwart partisan to head the committee. Bob Livingston (R-LA) had contributed over $165,000 to the party and to party candidates (more than anyone else returning to the committee) and had a strong record of party support in previous Congresses. Although Gingrich generally followed seniority in distributing committee gavels in the 104th Congress, on Appropriations he elevated Livingston over three more senior legislators to ensure that the right person was at the helm of this critical committee. The pattern of emphasizing party loyalty (demonstrated through fund-raising and voting unity), even at the expense of following seniority, has continued since. When the Appropriations chair was filled most recently (in the 109th Congress), Jerry Lewis (R-CA) won with an average party unity score just above that of the most senior candidate, Ralph Regula (R-OH). Additionally, Lewis's fund-raising levels were nearly double those of Regula's; as a result, leadership selected a chair with less seniority than Regula for the second time since 1994.[3] Lewis himself suggested that party leaders got their wishes by choosing him when he said, just after winning the position, "I intend to lead a committee that is dedicated to fiscal restraint and committed to being an integral part of our Republican leadership's effort to rein in spending and balance the federal budget" (Schatz 2005, 71).

Given the decentralized norms of the committee, controlling the chair is not enough. A pathbreaking study by Heberlig (2003) shows that party leaders who control committee assignments are more likely to grant positions on prestige committees (including Appropriations) to legislators who demonstrate party loyalty through fund-raising and voting unity. Notwithstanding demonstrated efforts of Republicans to place party loyalists as the chairs of the full committee and as members of the committee, the loci of power in the Appropriations Committee are the subcommittee chairs. To what extent have Republican Party leaders been effective in naming party loyalists to these positions?

The Republican Party grants broad latitude to most committee chairs in selecting subcommittee chairs for their committees. The chair of the full Appropriations Committee has generally chosen subcommittee chairs on the basis of subcommittee seniority. The fact that the Appropriations Committee chairs have been "handpicked" by Republican leadership must certainly lead to subcommittee chairs on Appropriations being named in accordance with the wishes of party leadership. The characteristics that party leaders value are surely made clear to the full committee chair (because to become the Appropriations Committee chair one must already have met those criteria). After some setbacks in cutting spending during the appropriations process in 2002, Republican leaders made it clear that the voting loyalty of the cardinals was a requirement—party leaders spearheaded a successful move to change the rules of the House Republican Conference that would require the Appropriations chair's picks for subcommittee chair positions to be approved by the speaker-dominated Republican Steering Committee and by the full Republican Conference. To date, the Steering Committee has always accepted the subcommittee chairs proposed by the Appropriations chair. This could be a sign that the change in the method of selection was simply a formality. However, it could be that the Appropriations chair just chooses candidates who are certain to pass muster with the leadership.

Under either selection regime (chair-appointed or chair-appointed with Steering approval), there are clear avenues of influence for majority party leadership on the selection of appropriations subcommittee chairs. The conditional party government theory predicts that because the Republican caucus has become more homogeneous, it is very likely that they have greater ability to influence the selection of the cardinals. This chapter not only tests the hypothesis that Republican Party leaders were able to influence the process of chair selection (as suggested by conditional party government theory), but also that party leaders use their ability to influence subcommittee chair selection to encourage would-be cardinals to support party goals. The exchange theory predicts that Republican leadership should use the ability to select these chairs (if it exists) to further the goals of the party. We now turn to the development of testable hypotheses that can be drawn that would, if proven correct, support both the exchange theory and the conditional party government theory.

Hypotheses and Data

Drawing on the framework developed earlier in this book, we recall that political parties work for two principle goals: majority status (which requires a great deal of money) and passage of party-preferred policies (which requires relatively unified voting of party members, especially in the presence of slim majorities). Party leaders may offer the incentive of an Appropriations subcommittee chair position to legislators as a "prize" for members of the Appropriations Committee who distinguish themselves with strong fund-raising efforts and a record of using their legislative powers to support the party. Accordingly, the model predicting the winner of a subcommittee chair contest will include variables for the amount of *contributions* to the party and to party candidates (in thousands of dollars) and the candidates' *party unity* scores (the percentage of the time legislators vote with their party on votes where a majority of one party votes against a majority of the other party). Under the exchange theory, we should expect that a member with higher levels of fund-raising and party unity should have a greater probability of winning a subcommittee chair position on Appropriations.

Notwithstanding the powers that party leaders may exert on the selection process, it may be that party leaders still cannot overcome the peculiar culture of the Appropriations Committee. One indicator of the extent to which the party has not completely subverted the culture of the committee is the extent to which seniority is used in allocating subcommittee chair positions. Senior legislators on Appropriations tend to be more entrenched in the spendthrift culture of the committee, a tendency that works against the wishes of House Republican leadership.

The historically strict seniority tradition of the Democratic Party on the Appropriations Committee allocates positions on the basis of *subcommittee seniority*. A compromise position between the party leadership and the committee might be to use *full committee seniority* as a factor rather than subcommittee seniority. Using full committee seniority honors the specialization of longtime members of the committee while also allowing Republican leadership a wider selection of possible subcommittee chairs from which they can choose a member who might also be more ideologically acceptable. Further, this frees Republican leaders to switch subcommittee chairs who have performed to the liking of party leadership to the chair of a different subcommittee after they are term-limited out of their first subcommittee chairship, even if that chair has little seniority on other subcommittees. Accordingly, the model will include variables for subcommittee seniority and seniority on Appropriations. Conditional party government theory would predict that both types of seniority (but especially subcommittee seniority) should be ideally unrelated the probability of winning a chair because of the strong, homogeneous majority party in the 107th and 108th Congresses. However, it may be that party leaders have increased their influence but have not fully dismissed seniority in selecting subcommittee chairs.

A second possible indicator that the culture of Appropriations still trumps the power of party leaders is the role that the Appropriations chair plays in the selection process. Rather than promoting partisan loyalty, it may be that the selection process favors subcommittee chair candidates who are ideologically proximate to the Appropriations Committee chair. Thus, it seems appropriate to include a control for ideological similarity to the chair. This variable, *ideological distance* from the chair, is measured as the absolute difference between the first dimension DW-NOMINATE score of the full Appropriations Committee chair and the first dimension DW-NOMINATE score for each Appropriations Committee member. Conditional party government theory would predict that ideological distance from the chair should be unrelated to the probability of winning a subcommittee chair position. The rationale for this is that the party will look for subcommittee chairs who are loyal to the party, not to the chair. Thus, in concert with the variable on party support, this variable allows us to test (in part) whether it is the Appropriations Committee chair that controls the process or the leadership-dominated Steering Committee.

Data and Results

These hypotheses will be tested on open seats for subcommittee chairs on the Appropriations Subcommittees of the 107th and 108th Congresses. These Congresses are chosen because there are many seats filled in this time period due to the term limits on subcommittee chairs that generated a great deal of turnover.[4] As in chapter 5, the data will be analyzed with a Bayesian conditional logit model to address the fact that there are only a specific number of subcommittee committee chair positions available.[5] Non-freshman majority-party members who do not hold a higher leadership position are considered in the dataset. The field of candidates for each subcommittee chair is determined by the subcommittee roster from the previous Congress.

Results of the statistical model appear in Table 6.1. While the results do not come down decisively in favor of the party, it is evident that party leaders do exert substantial influence on the process, offering a reasonable amount of support for both the conditional party government and exchange theories. By all accounts, the Appropriations Committee historically gives substantial deference to seniority (Fenno 1966, White 1989). These results show that seniority on the full committee indeed has a substantial, positive effect on the probability of winning a subcommittee chair position, but that subcommittee seniority actually *decreases* the likelihood of obtaining a subcommittee chair.

TABLE 6.1 Conditional Logit Model of Appropriations Subcommittee Chair Selection

	Coefficient (95% HPD Interval)
Contributions (in thousands)	.029* (.008, .052)
Party Unity	−.027 (−.224, .176)
Ideological Distance from Chair	−.026 (−.306, .246)
Subcommittee Seniority	−.713* (−1.181, −.268)
Full Committee Seniority	.846* (.433, 1.280)
% Correctly Predicted	75.0%
Number of Races	20
Number of Candidates	137

NOTE: Coefficients are posterior means.

*Denotes coefficients for which the 95% HPD interval does not contain 0.

SOURCE: Federal Election Commission, http://www.voteview.com, various issues of *CQ Weekly Report*, and the CQ Almanac.

Squaring this result with theories of partisan influence requires some extensive consideration. If party leaders were constrained to still count seniority as a factor, they would almost certainly prefer to emphasize full committee seniority rather than subcommittee seniority. Such an arrangement gives party leaders a wider base of candidates to choose from (senior members of the full committee rather than just those on a specific subcommittee). Additionally, with term limits being in effect, party leaders sometimes assign a member who has effectively chaired a subcommittee for six years to move to the chair of a different subcommittee on which they have substantially less seniority. This enables the party to keep subcommittee chairs who are supportive of the party in a position of power while also honoring the norm of full committee seniority (but essentially ignoring the role of subcommittee seniority). These two points may explain the party's willingness to honor full committee seniority, but a third point is in order in regards to the negative sign on subcommittee seniority. A member who has served on a committee for a number of terms but has not been chosen by the party (whatever the reason—little fund-raising, personal factors, etc.) will always continue to build subcommittee seniority unless removed from the committee (an unlikely event). However, such a member would have increasingly slim chances of ever being named as a chair. Thus, once one controls for full committee seniority, subcommittee seniority may actually have a negative effect.

The fact that parties at least influence subcommittee committee chair selection is also strongly supported by the finding that more party fund-raising (contributions to candidates and party committees) increases the likelihood of securing a subcommittee chair position. In contrast, party unity does not seem to have a significant effect on the probability of winning. One possible explanation lies in the criteria used to select members of the full committee. Heberlig (2003) showed that party unity was an important determinant of selection to the Appropriations Committee. Taking the results at hand in combination with Heberlig's work one can find a suitable explanation. It seems that the party is so careful in choosing who sits on the Appropriations Committee in the first place, that less ideological filtering would be necessary in choosing someone to chair the subcommittees. Indeed, the mean party unity score for Republican members of the Appropriations Committee in the 107th and 108th Congresses is over 90! In short, there are enough ideologically acceptable members on the committee that the party, even though it can exert power on the selection process, can choose from any number of ideologically appropriate individuals. In contrast, helping with party fund-raising is something that members must do each election cycle, and the party may use these positions to encourage perpetual fund-raising efforts. Taken together, these coefficients on fund-raising and party unity offer at least moderate levels of support for the exchange theory.

Results are quite clear that the chair of the full Appropriations Committee does not select subcommittee chairs on the basis of ideological proximity.[6] Instead, the Appropriations chair seems to select candidates in accordance with the wishes of party leaders, balancing support of party goals and full committee seniority.

Discussion

This chapter began with a discussion of the power of the subcommittee chairs on the Appropriations Committee. Aldrich and Rohde (2000) contended that in concordance with the theory of conditional party government, Republican leaders have received greater powers from the membership and that they have used those powers to reform the House Appropriations Committee. While Aldrich and Rohde focused largely on the legislative powers of the committee, this chapter has considered the power to control the subcommittee leadership selection process.

In chapter 5, we saw that Republican leaders have effectively taken control of the leadership selection process for full committee chairs and dismantled the traditional seniority system. The leaders use their control over that process to provide incentives for members of Congress to increase their voting support of party members and especially to raise funds for the party and party candidates. The evidence in this chapter does suggest that party leaders have successfully altered the subcommittee chair selection process to work in their favor. Most particularly, we see that party leaders use Appropriations subcommittee chair positions to foster fund-raising on the part of subcommittee chair aspirants. Leaders place greater expectations on those who hold these positions precisely because they hold an office with a sufficiently high profile as to be able to attract a higher volume of contributions from individuals and from PACs.

Nevertheless, the transformation wrought by leaders on the selection of Appropriations Subcommittee chairs is not as complete as that of full committee chairs discussed in chapter 5. Full committee seniority remains an important factor in selecting subcommittee chairs on Appropriations. While the party can be flexible and work around this norm to achieve its goals, the fact that the seniority norm has thus far proven insurmountable suggests that the party has not completely been able to replace the culture and norms of the Appropriations Committee with a party-driven mode of operation.

On the New Culture of the Appropriations Committee

The fact that the party has made significant inroads (but not completely infiltrated the culture of the committee) seems to have fueled additional efforts to reform the Appropriations Committee. In the 109th Congress, Lewis won the full committee chair position after donating nearly $2 million and campaigning on a promise to work to reform the Appropriations Committee. Following his selection, Lewis endorsed a plan developed by Tom DeLay to reduce the number of subcommittees on Appropriations and to shuffle the jurisdictions. The appropriators fought hard against the reforms, with the Senate Appropriations Committee weighing in out of fear that their committee would also be attacked by party leaders. While the battle took several months, eventually a compromise was reached that whittled the number of Appropriations subcommittees from 13 to 10, eliminating committees with interests and spending habits contrary to the preferences of the Republican leadership. Lewis made his intentions to fight for a more partisan culture on the committee clear in a statement made shortly after his appointment as chair: "We have a historic opportunity and a unique responsibility to reform the appropriations process and change the culture of the committee" (Schatz 2005, 71).

The fact that Republican Party leaders were able to make reforms was itself important; it seems that an increasingly active party leadership has been successful in diminishing the nonpartisan culture of the Appropriations Committee. As parties become increasingly pressed for greater amounts of funding, members may be willing to grant even more power to party leaders to select subcommittee leadership on Appropriations (and potentially on other committees) in such a way as to help raise additional funds.

Democrats and the 110th Congress

House Democratic Caucus rules traditionally allow members to bid for appropriations subcommittee leadership positions in the order of seniority on the subcommittee. Like with committee chair appointments, Democrats chose to generally revert to the norm of seniority for their first term back in power. However, while seniority was followed in most instances, the new chair of the reinstated Subcommittee on the Legislative Branch, Debbie Wasserman Schultz (D-FL) did not even hold a position on the Appropriations Committee prior to being named as chair, and the appointment came at the beginning of her second term in the House of Representatives. No doubt her solid liberal credentials and $366,400 in contributions to Democratic Party committees and to Democratic candidates bolstered her support among party leaders. In short, while Democrats may have given more credence to seniority than Republicans in recent Congresses, fund-raising still matters for House Democrats.

CHAPTER 7

Member Contributions
and the Politics of Party
Leadership Selection

The Constitution specifies only one official leadership position for the House of Representatives: The Speaker of the House. However, both parties select additional leadership, such as the minority/majority leader and minority/majority whip, to help accomplish legislative goals. These additional party leaders, selected by secret ballot within party caucuses, exert tremendous influence on the policy process. Indeed, for the party that does not control the presidency, congressional leaders are the highest-ranking elected officials within a party, thus taking on significant national leadership roles.

Given the considerable power vested in party leaders, it is surprising how little attention has been paid to the selection of congressional party leaders. Perhaps the paucity of scholarship in this arena is due to the secretive nature of the process. The votes for leadership positions are conducted with complete anonymity, and while many members publicly pledge their support to one candidate or another, the final vote counts show that in many cases, a significant number of individuals violated their pledge (though it is, of course, never obvious which legislators waffled).

Existing accounts of leadership selection focus on a blend of factors, such as regional representation, seniority, ideological balance, and parliamentary expertise (Davidson and Oleszek 2004). No single factor from among these can adequately explain each outcome, though legislators appear to balance them when making their decisions (Peabody 1976). Still, a new factor appears to be taking center stage in party leadership contests—the ability to raise funds for the party and for party candidates. Heberlig, Hetherington, and Larson (2006) and Heberlig and Larson (2007) show that fund-raising is a key factor used by the core leadership (e.g., Speaker, majority/minority leader, majority/minority whip, and conference/caucus chair) in selecting members of Congress for low- and mid-level party leadership positions. While Heberlig, Hetherington, and Larson present some evidence that fund-raising has grown in importance for core leadership positions, the effect relative to other considerations in selecting core leaders is less clear.

I previously noted that leaders imposed fund-raising quotas on committee chairs; similar quotas have been established for senior party members. Party leaders, however, set the highest quotas for themselves (Herrnson 2004). Given the escalating costs of congressional campaigns, it seems logical that fund-raising for the party would be a critical factor in evaluating leadership candidates. Further, given that members of Congress select their leaders, it seems that leadership aspirants could use contributions to other members of Congress as a means to shore up support for future leadership bids. It would be easier to go to a member of Congress and ask for the favor of their vote in a leadership election if a leadership candidate had contributed to that member's campaign.

While other considerations have not been discarded, the exchange theory of party influence predicts that party leadership aspirants will be more likely to be successful when they help the party meet its fund-raising goals. After all, fund-raising has become one of the major duties of party leaders. I contend that fund-raising for the party and for party candidates has become a key consideration in selecting Congressional party leadership. Indeed, fund-raising is so critical that without a demonstration of such pecuniary prowess, a leadership candidate cannot succeed in advancing their goals. I illustrate this point with a detailed case study focused on Nancy Pelosi's 2004 campaign to become the House minority leader, with references to other relevant leadership campaigns.

The Campaign Begins

Dick Gephardt's announcement that he would seek the Democratic nomination in the 2004 race for the presidency surprised no one. Since losing the nomination to Michael Dukakis in the 1988 elections, Gephardt suppressed his presidential ambitions until he saw another strong opportunity for his candidacy. While everyone acknowledged that he would need to give up his seat in Congress if his presidential campaign took off, many were surprised by his announcement of November 6, 2002 that he would leave Congress to pursue his aspiration. Political pundits, however, noted that an alternative explanation for Gephardt's departure was disappointment with the Democratic seat loss in the midterm elections. Whatever the reason for his departure, Gephardt's departure tipped off a frenzied race for the top leadership position in the House Democratic Caucus.

Upon Gephardt's announcement, two candidates for the top Democratic post immediately threw their hats into the ring—Pelosi and Martin Frost. Pelosi, a sixty-two-year-old representative from San Francisco, began the race with an edge—she was the Democratic whip, the second-highest ranking Democrat in the House. While the Democrats traditionally slide the sitting leadership up one spot when a position opens on top, this system of promotion is not inviolable. Indeed, with Pelosi being one of the most liberal members of the House, it seemed that a more centrist candidate could run a viable campaign against her.

Martin Frost (D-TX) saw that opportunity and entered the race. At the end of the 107th Congress, Frost was to be term-limited out of the third-ranking position of the House Democrats, the Democratic caucus chair (the Democratic Caucus chair and vice-chair are limited to two terms of service). A pro-business southern Democrat, he saw an opportunity to vie for the votes of centrists in the party.

Over the short course of two days, these two candidates would battle to win the votes of at least 50 percent of the House Democratic Caucus, with votes turning on three issues: ideological positioning, seniority, and campaign contributions. At the end of the brief battle, Frost would find his campaign floundering and withdraw from the race. While two other contenders would enter, waging quixotic campaigns, Pelosi emerged with 177 votes from the 206 members of the House Democratic Caucus[1] (Jones 2002). Three key factors loomed large in Pelosi's successful campaign: ideological positioning, experience, and financial support of the party and party candidates.

Ideological Positioning

Given the poor performance of the Democrats in the 2002 midterms, and the attribution of that failure to the Republican's success on national security and on the war in Iraq, the candidates naturally staked out positions on the war. Pelosi's approach was to draw a marked distinction between her position (and the positions she thought the party should take) and the position of the Bush administration. Pelosi was the highest ranking Democrat to vote against the Iraq War (Sandalow 2002a).

In contrast, Frost argued that an aggressive approach to national security and Iraq was necessary. Because these issues had helped Republicans succeed, Frost felt that by espousing similar views, he could steal the Republicans' thunder and bring the party back to strength. Fellow Texan Chet Edwards applauded Frost's position, saying, "In districts such as mine and for other moderate Democrats around the country, it will be important that Democratic leaders be seen as strong on national defense and national security issues, and on those issues I think Martin has a solid record" (Lindell 2002).

On other issues, as well as more generally, a similar pattern ensued. Pelosi was insistent that the best way for Democrats to rebuild after the Republicans' history-defying seat gain in the 2002 midterms was to move the party to the left. Distinguishing themselves from the policies of the Bush administration offered the only possibility to win back votes that had gone to Republicans in the midterm. As political scientist Bill Connelly put it, Frost's direction could be viewed as "Bush Lite," while Pelosi provided a "clear alternative" to George W. Bush (Lindell 2002). Still, while some Democrats saw Frost as a threat to the very soul of the Democratic Party, the rift between moderates and liberals that has plagued the party for so long provided a natural base of support for Frost (Thomma 2002). Further, Frost contended that because the American electorate had moved to the right, the Democratic Party could not find increased success by moving to the left (Sandalow 2002a).

Not only did the candidates clearly define their differences on the issues, but they also took very different approaches to broadcasting their positions. Frost made public appeals, appearing on television and trying to publicize his campaign message. After all, if Frost was going to succeed with his approach, he would need to show his colleagues that he had public support. In contrast, Pelosi kept a lower public profile, and sat down with a telephone and began a thirty-six-hour telephone marathon to ask for the support of those who would actually cast the votes—the 206 House Democrats. Pelosi made many of the calls directly—congratulating the representatives on their election, and asking for their support in her bid to succeed Gephardt. Additionally, Pelosi had an ideologically and regionally diverse team of colleagues placing calls on her behalf (Sandalow 2002b).

Ultimately, Pelosi's work resulted in a list of 110 names of pledged supporters (Wallison 2002). History has proven that in secret-ballot leadership elections, pledged supporters can be fickle. In 1976, Phil Burton (who ironically also represented San Francisco) claimed to have collected enough pledges of support from colleagues to win a race for Democratic majority leader. But when the final votes came in, he lost by one vote to Jim Wright (Sandalow 2001). However, in Pelosi's instance, history did not repeat itself. Frost believed that she had the votes, and withdrew from the race.

Experience

When replacing a vacancy on the Congressional leadership ladder, both parties, but more particularly the Democrats, have a pattern of promoting up the ladder, but that has increasingly diminished in recent years. On the Republican side, Dennis Hastert was a mid-level officer in the whip system when he was appointed as Speaker of the House. Additionally, since the Democrats made the whip an elective office in 1986 (rather than appointed by the Speaker and majority leader), Pelosi has been the only whip to move to a higher position. In contrast, 6 of 10 Democratic whips appointed in the post-war period 1946–1986 moved on to higher House leadership positions (Foerstel 2001).

While Pelosi outranked the other candidates, it seemed to have little effect on the outcome of the minority leader race. None of the candidates (even Pelosi) claimed that they were "entitled" to the position by virtue of seniority in the way that many committee chair candidates historically have. Further, years of service in the House seemed to be of little value. While experience became a matter after Frost left the race and the relatively young Harold Ford (D-TN) entered the race, seniority did not loom large in the real contest between Frost and Pelosi.

Fund-raising and Financial Support
for Democratic Candidates

Simply on the basis of issue positioning, one can construct a plausible explanation for Pelosi's success in the 2002 minority leader election. However, to do so would omit one of the central reasons why people were willing to publicly pledge their support to Pelosi: fund-raising. If the election were about ideology, then Frost should have won the support of moderates, and Pelosi would have secured support only from the left side of the party. However, Pelosi proudly announced the support of moderates like John Murtha (D-PA), Lloyd Doggett (D-TX), Max Sandlin (D-TX), and Jan Schakowsky (D-IL). Not only did moderates publicly endorse her, but they even campaigned on her behalf (Sandalow 2002b). With leadership seniority being violable, why would moderates ever support Pelosi? Over the course of the 2002 election cycle, Pelosi gave over one million reasons—each one a dollar—to Democratic candidates across all regions and ideologies. Further, she doled out another $642,000 in contributions to Democratic Party committees.

Fund-raising at two different time points generated Pelosi's swift success. First, she worked as a fund-raiser even before she knew she was in a race. While it was known that Gephardt would eventually vacate his post at the helm of the House Democratic Party, no one was certain when that would happen. Accordingly, Pelosi raised funds as though she was already in a race. Thus, when Gephardt announced his resignation, Pelosi was prepared to call on those whom she had supported for reciprocation. Not having anticipated the minority leader vacancy (and being term limited from his party leadership position), Frost distributed only about half as much in contributions as Pelosi did. When the vacancy appeared, the campaign season had just ended, and it was too late to make additional contributions.[2]

Second, members still remembered the remarkable fund-raising campaign Pelosi waged when she ran for the Democratic whip position in 2001. Of the relationship between fund-raising and victory in the bitterly fought whip race against Stenny Hoyer (D-MD) one of Pelosi's aides noted, "It took us three years to win the whip's race, and 36 hours to win this [minority leader race]" (Sandalow 2002b).

In some sense, the campaign for the whip position really began in the 2000 election cycle. Democrats believed that they would take control of the House, meaning that Gephardt would become the Speaker and Minority Whip David Bonior (D-MI) would be elevated to majority leader. That would leave a vacancy in the whip position, which Pelosi and Hoyer both had their eyes on. Though the Democrats' aspiration of re-taking the House never materialized, the possibility set off the Pelosi/Hoyer race.

Ultimately, the campaigning that had seemed premature revived when sitting whip David Bonior announced his gubernatorial candidacy just over a year later. Accordingly, Pelosi and Hoyer again jumped on the fund-raising trail, making contributions to shore up support for their leadership bids. Pelosi out-raised and out-donated Hoyer by several hundred thousand dollars. After contacting members of the caucus for pledges of support, Pelosi claimed 120 supporters, while Hoyer claimed 105. However, with about a dozen uncommitted members, and only 226 caucus members (counting the 5 delegates and Bernard Sanders [I-VT] who caucuses with the Democrats), it was clear that either Pelosi or Hoyer (or both) had miscalculated their true level of support. As noted earlier, members of Congress are notoriously fickle in the secret ballot elections for party leadership. In any case, it was clear that Hoyer was counting on picking up most of the members who publicly announced that they were undecided.

Hoyer was not as fortunate as he had hoped he would be. When the votes were counted, Pelosi was the victor, 118–95 (Foerstel 2001). It appears that the coalition of support that Pelosi built in the whip's race laid a solid foundation of support for her in her bid for minority leader just over a year later.[3]

Pelosi's fund-raising work is effective in part because rather than donating to candidates who ask for help, she makes direct offers of assistance. Loretta Sanchez (D-CA) recalls that before she even knew Pelosi's name, Pelosi called her, saying that if Sanchez could spare a little time away from her district she would raise $40,000 for her. Ultimately, Pelosi raised over $80,000 for her (Martinez 2002). Pelosi has even applied innovative campaign finance techniques to raise money for other members. When Mike Ross (D-AR) challenged an incumbent Republican, Jay Dickey, Pelosi used a technique known as "bundling" to raise money for Ross. In addition to contributions from her own funds, Pelosi found contributors in her network who were willing to write checks directly to Ross. However, rather than having the donors mail their checks to Ross, she collected them and presented her collective efforts on his behalf directly to him to underscore the level of support she had generated for his campaign (Cook 2001).

Aftermath

Within two days of Gephardt's announcement, the "real" race was run and won. Even though the official vote would not be taken for several weeks, Pelosi felt confident in her victory after Frost withdrew from the race. A small coalition of Democrats, however, was disappointed when Frost withdrew because they saw his message of moderation as the most promising direction for their party. This void inspired blue dog Harold Ford (D-TN) to enter the race. Further, Rep. Marci Kaptur (D-OH) threw her hat into the ring.

It is hard to believe that Kaptur really thought she could win the top post, but it seems more likely that she ran to try to promote reforms in government and in the caucus (Evote 2002). However, her campaign generated little attention, probably because she was not seen as a serious contender, and also because the media attention at this point in the race focused on the slightly more serious challenge posed by Ford.

Ford picked up the banner of moderation and campaigned for the support of the Democrats who saw Pelosi as too far left of center. Ford had little time to make contributions and to try to gain support. Anna Eshoo, one of Pelosi's California colleagues, accused Ford of running to raise his profile and to try to gain power in the House (Grove 2002).

When asked about Ford's challenge, Pelosi simply noted, "I'm not concerned about it" (Lee 2002). Her confidence was well founded. Though Ford had the ideological message of moderation that had made Frost a real contender, he had not made the contributions to other candidates that Pelosi had made. Pelosi ended up with 177 votes to Ford's 29 (Sandalow 2002b).

Additional Factors, Balance in Leadership Selection, and Fund-raising: Why the Exchange Theory Matters

Even in a case study, it is difficult to consider all of the possible factors related to the selection of a congressional leader. Peabody's (1976) seminal study of leadership selection lists about twenty factors that parties consider in selecting leadership (though fund-raising is not among them). While no candidate will meet every criterion, a team of leadership should collectively hold most, if not all, of the key attributes that Peabody outlines. Sinclair (1995) emphasizes the importance of a diverse leadership team that draws from various subgroups within parties. These claims taken together outline one of the overarching themes of leadership selection: An effective party leadership team will be balanced in such a way that they represent the party and collectively possess critical leadership attributes (see also Sinclair 1983, Canon 1989, Heberlig and Larson 2007).

In discussing the 2001 leadership races (Pelosi vs. Hoyer for Democratic whip and Menendez vs. DeLauro for caucus chair), we noted balancing of gender and ideology as factors leading to the selection of Menendez over DeLauro. However, a similar balance on both of these dimensions could have been reached by selecting DeLauro as caucus chair and Hoyer as whip. Why, then, did we observe the caucus selecting one combination over another?

Many attributes of leadership selection require balancing. Parties strive to appoint some leaders from the north, some from the south, some from large states, some from small states, some male, some female, some media savvy opinion leaders, others veterans at the inner politicking of Congress, some white, some nonwhite. However, parties feel no compulsion to balance the appointment of a prolific party benefactor with a lackluster fund-raiser. Pelosi and Menendez exhibited a fund-raising capacity beyond their competitors, making the choice a relatively straightforward one for party members. Exchange theory predicts that as fund-raising increases in importance to the party, the expectations for fund-raising by leadership aspirants will continue to rise until they reach a point where the value of the leadership position exceeds the effort required to raise the requisite level of funding. As long as there are members who are willing to raise ever-larger amounts of money for the party and party candidates, fund-raising expectations will continue to grow (assuming majority control of Congress continues to be in play). Particularly in a period marked by intense battles for majority control of Congress, it should come as no surprise that empirical studies show that fund-raising has become more important than ideological balancing (Heberlig, Hetherington, and Larson 2006) and descriptive representation (Heberlig and Larson 2007) in selecting party leaders.

Discussion

Members of Congress acknowledge the critical value of campaign support in winning leadership elections. Rep. Barney Frank (D-MA) said of Pelosi, "Nancy is first-rate. She's a great fund-raiser, but she's as committed on issues as anyone. It looks like fund-raising will always be with us . . . so it's important to have a noncorrupt fund-raiser committed to the core values of liberalism" (Nolan 2001).

While seniority and experience seem to be important (all of the serious contenders in the leadership races examined here had it), one candidate having a greater degree than the other was not determinative of success. While there is an element of ladder-climbing to leadership selection, history is replete with examples of those who have skipped rungs.

Ideology continually surfaces as an issue in leadership campaigns. Moderate members seek to be represented in leadership, while more conventional party members hope to choose someone committed to the core values of liberalism or conservatism. In all three cases discussed here (Pelosi vs. Frost, Pelosi vs. Hoyer, and DeLauro vs. Menendez) and in most cases through history where leadership races have been contested, one candidate claims to be able to lead the party in a better ideological direction than the other. However, in the three races considered here, ideology is not determinative. In both Pelosi races, the committed liberal succeeded; however, in the Menendez versus DeLauro race, the moderate emerged as the victor.

While it may appear that commitment to party ideology aided Pelosi in her victories, there is something unsatisfying about promoting ideology as the best explanation for success in leadership elections. Indeed, DeLauro and Pelosi shared a common ideology, but DeLauro lost her 2002 bid for Democratic Caucus chair, while Pelosi succeeded in her race. Report after report on the races consider Pelosi's ideology as being a potential liability as much an asset to her campaigns (Cook 2001, Lindell 2002, Sandalow 2002a, Thomma 2002). Indeed, Pelosi herself discounted the importance of the ideology factor, saying, "It's not about advocating any point of view. It's about serving as a leader" (Foerstel 2001).

Conclusion

While these three recent races for Democratic leadership positions do not suggest that ideology determines the outcomes of leadership races, they offer strong support for the hypothesis that fund-raising is essential for waging a successful leadership campaign. This is particularly the case because unlike other attributes that require balancing, parties seek fund-raising skills in all leadership candidates. It is unlikely that either party will ever elect a leader who does not first demonstrate a strong capacity as a fund-raiser. As campaigns become more expensive, and as reforms (e.g, the BCRA) make money scarce, leadership support through fund-raising will only become more important.

Two questions remain for future research. First, this chapter has focused on the role of fund-raising in Democratic House leadership elections. This must be expanded on two frontiers. Future work must examine the role of fund-raising in Republican leadership selection. At first glance, this appears to be the case—In the 2002 elections, Roy Blunt (R-MO) pitched over $600,000 into party coffers and into the campaigns of fellow candidates. He was rewarded with the Republican whip position (Bedlington and Malbin 2003). In the six years prior to the 2006 Republican majority leader contest, John Boehner gave $3.3 million[4] to Republican Party committees and to Republican candidates while Blunt raised $3.6 million. The fact that Boehner won suggests that once some level of fund-raising ability has been demonstrated, other factors remain influential (in this case, Blunt's strong ties to ex-Majority Leader Tom DeLay). However, it is noteworthy that John Shadegg (R-AZ), who raised and redistributed only about one-tenth of Boehner or Blunt's contributions, was eliminated after winning only forty votes on the first ballot. In addition to exploring the role of fund-raising in leadership elections for both parties, the effect of fund-raising on leadership elections in the Senate should be investigated.

Second, larger-n empirical analyses of leadership races could help to better quantify the effects of fund-raising, ideology, and other factors. Heberlig, Hetherington, and Larson (2006) make an important move in this direction, showing that successful leadership candidates certainly raise more money in recent years than they did before the 104th Congress. However, more research is needed to specifically link the increased levels of fund-raising to success in leadership races while also controlling for other factors.

CHAPTER 8

Conclusion

The data in chapter 2 show that member-to-member and member-to-party contributions are increasing in size and importance. As previously noted, however, a growing source of campaign funds is relatively unimportant unless it has observable implications. The results presented in this book strongly support the conclusion that member-to-member and member-to-party contributions have significant political consequences for legislative voting, and for committee and party leadership selection. However, these effects are all tied to the strengthening of parties via strategic exchanges that mobilize party members to help reach collective party goals. Given the far-reaching effects of member contributions, it seems appropriate to reflect on the normative and institutional ramifications of these contributions.

Institutional Consequences

In the beginning, this book set out to show that as parties help the members meet their political ambitions, members will respond by supporting party positions. Party leaders help members meet their electoral goals by making contributions to support their reelection. In return, rank-and-file party members vote more frequently in support of the party. Party leaders help members meet their goal to gain power in Washington by allocating committee and party leadership positions. However, those positions are only granted in exchange for support of the party (ideologically and financially). Increasingly, member contributions constitute the currency that runs through the exchanges that shape the contemporary Congress.

Two overall institutional consequences can be drawn from the conclusions of chapters 4–7. First, the political parties have restructured the basis for selecting leadership. Fund-raising on behalf of other candidates and party committees has become so essential that members of Congress who seek committee chair, subcommittee chair, and party leadership positions are unlikely be successful without demonstrating their fund-raising capacity. The former criteria (seniority and ideology) have taken a backseat to fund-raising abilities. This constitutes a significant shift in the organization of Congress. The changes in Congress as an institution due to the rise of leader contributions are as sweeping as the reforms of Congress at the time of the revolt against Cannon and the congressional reforms of the 1970s. Second, both the use of member contributions to increase loyalty and the exchange of committee and party leadership seats for financial contributions have increased party unity in the House. The demonstrated effectiveness of these exchanges for building party unity affirms that political parties have tremendous influence on the operation of the U.S. Congress.

The exchange theory of party influence enhances our understanding of partisan influence in Congress without contradicting the fundamental tenets of current theories of party effects in Congress. Proponents of the conditional party government hypothesis contend that congressional party strength comes when members of the party are internally ideologically cohesive and also ideologically distinct from the opposing party. Such an arrangement allows members of Congress to safely delegate some of their decision-making power to party leaders. To be sure, some of the commodities exchanged by party leaders (e.g., committee and subcommittee chair positions) are only available to them when the conditions of conditional party government are met. In these circumstances, the exchange theory adds to the conditional party government approach by more clearly specifying what party leaders do to influence members when the conditions for partisan influence prevail.

Scholars who maintain that the strength of parties is more constant than the conditional party government theory allows (e.g., Cox and McCubbins 1993, 2005) will be satisfied to note that these exchanges may operate using commodities available to party leaders regardless of the distribution of preferences in the chamber. Party leaders can offer campaign contributions and leadership positions in return for support on the party's legislative interests. Leader contributions are as important in campaign financing today as innovative campaign finance techniques like party independent expenditures and contribution bundling. The presence of these exchanges may also add to the party cartel approach. While party cartel theory predicts that party leaders can structure votes in such a way as to ensure that the majority party is not "rolled" (a bill passes that the majority opposes), exchanges between party and party members enable party leaders to bolster their positive powers (the ability to pass legislation that the majority supports). As such, the exchange theory fits well within recent research on the strength of parties within Congress.

A host of other possible exchanges exist that may be explored in the context of the exchange, conditional party government, and party cartel theories. Research has shown that members of Congress seek distributive benefits for their district, and that federal spending is not spread equally or randomly across districts (e.g., Stein and Bickers 1995; Bickers and Stein 2000). It may be that party leaders work to send more pork to the districts of rank-and-file members of Congress who raise more money for the party. Additionally, thousands of bills are introduced in each Congress, but only a fraction are ever debated and voted on. It may be that party leaders use their procedural powers to bring legislation to the floor that was sponsored by members of Congress who raise substantial funds for the party. Many more possibilities exist, all of which fall squarely under the exchange theory, but that must be left to a future day for full investigation.

Normative Consequences

Normative Implications of the Institutional Consequences

While the institutional consequences of member contributions are clear, the normative implications are never as simple. Many political scientists have long championed a disciplined party system as an improvement to the American polity. Indeed, in a rare move, the American Political Science Association (1950) issued a lengthy report on the benefits of a more responsible party system. Stronger parties, the report notes, create a system more resistant to pressure groups. Where members are receiving their campaign funds from party leaders instead of from special interests, there would be less concern about interest groups "buying" influence in Congress. Further, the report contends that voters would be given a clear choice between two alternatives under a strong party system. Finally, the report contends that under a strong party system, parties are responsible for their actions. In a system with decentralized power, it is difficult to assign credit or blame. However, under a strong party system, it is clear which members advocate which policies, so voters can easily hold their representative accountable.

In spite of the enthusiasm of mid-twentieth century political scientists, strong party systems come with negative effects as well. While a strong party system creates two clear choices, it creates only two choices. Heterogeneous, moderate districts would be faced with choosing between two candidates who would represent the district poorly if they were required to support party positions. Additionally, political power is centered in the hands of a few individuals. Finally, while contributions from party leaders may free legislators from their bonds to special interests, they still owe "favor debts" to party leaders. For some, it makes little difference whether members are pulled away from supporting their constituency by special interests or party leaders—the constituency still gets less representation. Ultimately, whether one regards the stronger-party implication of member contributions as good or bad depends on whether or not one favors strong parties.

The rise of fund-raising capacity as a determinant of committee chair selection has significant implications. The seniority system aimed to ensure that the most experienced and knowledgeable committee members chaired the committees. To select a good committee chair, the selection process must somehow ascertain the candidates' aptitude for the chair position. However, a member's fund-raising prowess has little to do with how well he or she can run a committee. Even party unity is not necessarily a good indication of how skilled a legislator would be as a committee chair. Further, to the extent that committee chairs simply echo the wishes of party leaders, an important source of information in the chamber is lost.

While the demise of seniority-determined chair appointments has drawbacks, it also has benefits. During the era of strong committee chairs, legislation that was supported by a majority in the chamber never came to a vote because strong committee chairs kept the legislation locked in committee. Making committee chairs responsible to party leaders and to the chamber as a whole makes the House, in at least this regard, more majoritarian.

Normative Implications of Behavioral Consequences

While the institutional consequences of member contributions have important normative implications, the fact that members are raising money itself has important implications. Individuals and groups make contributions to express support of a candidate, while that candidate may simply pass that money on to a different candidate (potentially even a candidate who the original donors would not support). Further, candidates who sponsor leadership PACs are able to double their fund-raising and donation activities. Members of Congress can give twice as much to other candidates by contributing the legal limit from their PAC and then giving the limit again from their personal campaign committee. This effective increase in the amount of money that members can give to other members increases the amount of influence they can gain with other members. Some scholars (notably Currinder 1998) have contended that essentially doubling these limits for members of Congress is unfair. Similarly, members can double the legal contribution limit from individuals and from PACs by accepting contributions to their personal campaign committee and to their leadership PAC. This practice, dubbed "double-dipping," raises fears that the individuals who have the most power over legislation (leadership PACs are most common among party leaders, committee chairs, and those who aspire to those positions) are more beholden to special-interest donors (Stone 1996). This proposition is yet to be empirically tested in a rigorous way. The implications of this possibility hinge on one's views on the value of strong political parties—For those who see strong parties and bridled committee chairs as a good way to govern, whatever consequences are generated by accepting additional PAC money may be a small price to pay.

Conclusion

Member contributions have skyrocketed since their introduction. In the contemporary Congress, they are an important component of exchanges between party leaders and rank-and-file legislators. In the wake of the fund-raising restrictions contained in the McCain-Feingold Bipartisan Campaign Reform Act of 2002, member contributions will only increase in size and importance as candidates scramble to assemble ever-larger sums of campaign money.

Member contributions have already profoundly affected the overall institutional operations of Congress. Members of Congress vote differently because of member contributions. Congressional leadership is selected differently because of member contributions and congressional elections work differently because of member contributions. Virtually every aspect of the functioning of Congress has already been affected by the rise of member contributions. As members look more and more to their parties for campaign funds (and as parties look more and more to their leaders and leadership aspirants to supply those funds), the consequences outlined herein will only become better defined.

Notes

Preface

1. A handful of non-incumbent candidates make some contributions, which might suggest a distinction between "candidate" contributions and member contributions. However, because there are relatively few candidate contributions that are not from members of Congress, and in keeping with existing literature on the topic, I use the terms *candidate contributions* and *member contributions* synonymously to refer to contributions from one candidate to another or from one candidate to their party.

Chapter 2

1. This timing is likely because Newt Gingrich's leadership PAC, GOPAC, was instrumental in taking control of the House in 1994. Given the evident success of that strategy, members have continued to redistribute more and more money since that election.

2. Campaign finance data used in this chapter were obtained from the FEC http://www.fec.gov, the Center for Responsive Politics http://www.crp.org, and from Michael Malbin.

3. A race is considered competitive if the candidate's vote total in the general election is between 40 and 60 percent.

4. Clearly, both of these relationships are potentially endogenous. Candidates may be successful in winning a primary because they received member contributions, or they may be competitive candidates in the general election because they received member contributions. Conversely, they may have received the contributions because they are likely primary winners or likely competitive candidates. In all likelihood, the causality runs in both directions. It is beyond the scope

of this chapter to resolve these issues. Rather, I simply intend to demonstrate a correlation between contributions, primary success, and competitiveness.

5. Note that in the 2000 elections, House Democrats were particularly hopeful that they could take control of the House, meaning advancement of someone (probably Gephardt) to Speaker, moving Bonior to majority leader, and opening the whip position. In preparation for that transition (which did not happen), many candidates made large contributions to party committees and to other members.

Chapter 3

1. The evidence that these excess funds deter potential challengers is limited; see Goodliffe (2001) and Ansolabehere and Snyder (2000) on this point.

2. It should be noted that others following in Krehbiel's wake have provided some evidence. For example, Jenkins (1999) compares the voting records of legislators who served in both the U.S. Congress (with party organizations) and Confederate Congresses (which had no parties) and found a significant party effect. Nokken (2000) compared individuals who switched parties but who kept the same constituencies and similarly finds party effects. Wright and Schaffner (2002) find strong party effects when comparing partisan and nonpartisan state legislatures.

3. Other possible selective incentives that I leave for later consideration include calendaring of bills and the allocation of pork projects.

Chapter 4

1. Because the model uses two lags of the contribution variables as instruments, the model can only incorporate legislators who served three or more consecutive terms during the 102nd–106th Congresses. Additionally, because of the lags, the results reflect outcomes in the 104th, 105th, and 106th Congresses. This makes for a more conservative test of the hypothesis that leadership contributions affect party unity because entrenched incumbents would be more difficult to persuade to support the party relative to freshmen.

2. When Republicans hold a majority in Congress, their top four offices are Speaker, majority leader, majority whip, Conference chair, and Policy Committee chair; for Democrats the top four offices are minority leader, minority whip, caucus chair, and caucus vice-chair. When Democrats control the House, their top four leaders are Speaker, majority leader, majority whip, and caucus chair; the top four Republican leaders are the minority leader, minority whip, Conference chair, and Policy Committee chair. The top four leaders make an

ideal set because they are actively engaged in encouraging loyalty on a wide range of issues for all legislators. Further, through most of this period, all four leaders of both parties sponsored leadership PACs, making the numbers comparable through the period. As one moves further down the leadership ranks in earlier time periods, fewer members of the extended leadership sponsored leadership PACs.

3. Note that factors that do not change over time or change at a constant rate are controlled for by the fixed-effects.

4. Because this model does not require the use of earlier time periods as instruments, the sample sizes for this model (as well as the comparison of means in Table 4.2) is larger than the model in Table 4.1. This implies that the relationship found earlier holds across an even broader time span.

Chapter 5

1. All seniority data presented in the chapter are based on the following sources: Polsby, Gallaher, and Rundquist (1969), Stewart and Woon's Congressional Committee Dataset, *Congressional Quarterly's Guide to Congress* (1994), and various issues of *Congressional Quarterly Weekly Report* listing the committee rosters.

2. Technically, the whole House must pass a resolution naming the full rosters of the committees, including the committee chairs. However, this is a formality and the members of the House have not tried to change the recommendations of the party leadership.

3. The model with separate variables for contributions to the party and to party candidates fits no better than the restricted model. Further, re-running the conditional logit model on the Brewer and Deering (2005) data (also used in Deering and Wahlbeck [2006]) allows us to test the null hypothesis that the different types of contributions all have the same effect. A statistical test of that hypothesis fails to reject the null, suggesting that aggregating the contributions is justifiable on statistical grounds.

4. For readers who may be concerned that some members of Congress may be familiar with works like Krehbiel (2000), leading those members to believe that party unity scores are not valid measures of party support, an additional point is in order. The Congressional Quarterly party unity score is generally criticized because it does not distinguish between members who are loyal to the party because of constituency preferences and members who are loyal to the party because of party pressure. In the instance of selecting a committee chair who will support party positions, party leaders would be indifferent when choosing between a chair who supports the party because he or she

has a Republican constituency and a chair who supports the party because he or she was led to by incentives or by personal attachments.

5. Three parallel chains ran for 110,000 iterations each with the first 10,000 iterations discarded as a burn-in. Point estimates are derived using posterior means and uncertainty is reflected using a 95 percent highest posterior density (HPD) interval. Priors on all coefficients were normal with mean 0 and variance 100. Alternative prior distribution specifications, such as uniform $(-5,5)$ made no substantive difference in the results.

6. Percent correctly predicted indicates the percentage of observed races where the actual winner of the race has a higher predicted probability of winning than any other candidate in the same race.

7. The DIC (Deviance Information Criterion) developed by Spiegelhalter, Best, Carlin, and van der Linde (2002) is a Bayesian method for assessing goodness of fit. It is particularly useful for comparing models. It is conceptually similar to the Akaike Information Criterion (AIC—Akaike 1973), estimating a posterior for the deviance statistic. Smaller DIC values indicate a better fit.

8. Results again are based on three parallel chains with each run for 110,000 iterations and the first 10,000 iterations discarded as a burn-in. Point estimates and HPDs are derived as discussed earlier. Priors on all coefficients were normal with mean 0 and variance 100. Alternative prior distribution specifications, such as uniform $(-5,5)$ made no substantive difference in the results.

9. Once again, results are based on three parallel chains with each run for 110,000 iterations and the first 10,000 iterations discarded as a burn-in. Point estimates and HPDs are derived as discussed earlier. Priors on all coefficients were normal with mean 0 and variance 100. Alternative prior distribution specifications, such as uniform $(-5,5)$ and a skeptical prior emphasizing a prior belief that seniority should matter (specifically Normal~$[1,1]$) made no substantive difference in the results.

10. For a discussion of the problems of dichotomizing "significance" especially when variables are quite close to the .05 cutoff, see Gelman and Stern (2005).

11. The predicted probabilities in Figure 5.3 are based on the relative seniority model in Table 5.5.

12. There were four races in this time period that were not contested: for the 107th Congress, Don Young for Transportation, Sherwood Boehlert for Science, and Jim Hansen for Natural Resources. In the 108th Congress, Duncan Hunter ran unopposed for the Armed Services Committee chair.

13. Mean committee seniority for committee chair candidates is 8.75, while it is about 4.3 for all members. The t-test is significant at $p < .01$.

14. Some may be concerned that excluding unopposed chair candidates may result in selection bias that favors candidates. However, I contend that unopposed chair candidates are not unopposed because of their level of seniority but rather because their levels of party unity and contributions to the party/party candidates are so high. This contention is supported by the qualitative discussion of the previous data.

15. Obey's official statement said that he had simply lost track of time and was late for the vote.

Chapter 6

1. It should be noted, however, that Aldrich and Rohde (2000) do devote some discussion to partisan stacking—they show that Republicans gave themselves a greater advantage in the ratio of Republicans to Democrats on the full committee and on the subcommittees for the size of their majority relative to the Democrats (for their size of majority) in the 103rd Congress.

2. It is also important to note that Aldrich and Rohde (2000) focus on the earlier years of the Republican era, before Republicans started placing as much emphasis on influencing the selection of Appropriations subcommittee chairs.

3. Bob Livingston (R-LA) was selected as the Appropriations Committee chair in the 104th Congress even though he was not the most senior member of the committee. C. W. Bill Young (R-FL), who chaired the committee for the 106th–108th Congresses, outranked Regula in seniority on the Appropriations Committee, so his selection did not constitute a violation of Regula's seniority.

4. The justification for using only open chair positions is also discussed in chapter 5, where the same approach is take to full committee chairs.

5. Three parallel chains ran for 110,000 iterations each, with the first 10,000 discarded as a burn-in. Both the Geweke and Gelman-Rubin diagnostics suggest convergence.

6. Re-running the model for just the 107th Congress makes no difference in the results here—even before subcommittee chairs required Steering Committee approval, the chair did not attempt to select subcommittee chairs who were ideologically proximate to himself.

Chapter 7

1. Note that delegates who do not have floor voting privileges still have voting rights in the Democratic Caucus, including voting rights in leadership elections.

2. It may be of interest to the reader to know that the race to fill the Democratic Caucus chair, which was known to be coming open because of term limits, showed a similar pattern of the importance of contributions. The winner, Bob Menendez (D-NJ), donated over $702,000 to Democratic candidates, while his opponent, Rosa DeLauro (D-CT) gave just under $40,000. Menendez ran with the same message of moderation as Frost, while DeLauro's ideology resembles Pelosi's. The common denominator that underscores these two cases (whether the opening was well-known beforehand or not) is campaign contributions.

3. It is worth noting that when Pelosi was promoted to minority leader, Stenny Hoyer ran unopposed for the whip position. Perhaps this is proof that an unsuccessful (but well-run) campaign for a leadership position may be rewarded with a leadership position later on.

4. Fund-raising numbers for the 2006 majority leader race are based on FEC reports.

References

Articles and Books

Abram, Michael E. and Joseph Cooper. 1968. The rise of seniority in the House of Representatives." *Polity* 1:52–85.

Akaike, Hirotugu, 1973. Information theory and an extension of the maximum likelihood principle. In *2nd International Symposium on Information Theory*, ed. B. N. Petrov and F. Csaki, 267–81. Budapest: Akademiai Kiado.

Aldrich, John H. 1995. *Why Parties? The Origin and Transformation of Party Politics in America*. Chicago: University of Chicago Press.

Aldrich, John H. and James S. Coleman Battista. 2002. Conditional party government in the states. *American Journal of Political Science* 46 (1): 164–72.

Aldrich, John H. and David W. Rohde. 2001. The logic of conditional party government. In *Congress Reconsidered*, eds. Lawrence C. Dodd and Bruce I. Oppenheimer. 269–92. Washington, DC: Congressional Quarterly Press.

———. 2000. The Republican Revolution and the House Appropriations Committee. *Journal of Politics* 62(1):1–33.

———. 1997–98. The transition to Republican rule in the House: Implications for theories of Congressional politics. *Political Science Quarterly* 112: 541–67.

Ansolabehere, Stephen and James Snyder. 2000. Campaign war chests in congressional elections. *Business and Politics* 2: 9–33.

APSA Committee on Political Parties. 1950. Toward a more responsible two-party system: A report of the Committee on Political Parties. *American Political Science Review* 44 (3, supple.): 1–100.

Baker, Ross. 1989. *The New Fat Cats: Members of Congress as Political Benefactors.* New York: Priority Press.

Bedlington, Anne and Michael Malbin. 2003. The party as an extended network: Members giving to each other and to their parties. In *Life after Reform,* ed. Michael Malbin, 124–40. Washington, DC: Campaign Finance Institute.

Bickers, Kenneth N. and Robert M. Stein. 2000. The congressional pork barrel in a Republican era. *Journal of Politics* 62: 1070–86.

Box-Steffensmeier, Janet. 1996. A dynamic analysis of the role of war chests in campaign strategy. *American Journal of Political Science* 40(May): 352–71.

Brady, David W., Joseph Cooper, and Patricia Hurley. 1979. The decline of party in the U.S. House of Representatives. *Legislative Studies Quarterly* 4(3): 381–407.

Brewer, Paul R. and Christopher J. Deering. 2005. Interest Groups, Campaign Fundraising, and Committee Chair Selection: House Republicans Play "Musical Chairs." In *The Interest Group Connection: Electioneering, Lobbying, and Policymaking in Washington,* eds. Paul S. Herrnson, Ronald G. Shaiko, and Clyde Wilcox, 144–63. New York: Chatham House Publishers

Buchler, Justin. 2002. The effect of leadership PAC contributions on party loyalty in the U.S. House. Paper presented at the 2002 annual meetings of the American Political Science Association, Boston.

Cann, Damon M. 2006. The decline of the seniority system in the U.S. House of Representatives. Paper presented at the Southern Political Science Association meetings, Atlanta.

Canon, David T. 1989. The institutionalization of leadership in the U.S. Congress. *Legislative Studies Quarterly* 14: 415–43.

Cantor, David M. and Paul S. Herrnson. 1997. Party campaign activity and party unity in the U.S. House of Representatives. *Legislative Studies Quarterly* 22: 393–415.

Caro, Robert A. 1983. *The Years of Lyndon Johnson: The Path to Power.* New York: Knopf.

Carson, Jamie L. 2005. Strategy, selection, and candidate competition in U.S. House and Senate elections. *Journal of Politics* 67(1):1–28.

Chappell, Henry W. 1982. Campaign contributions and Congressional voting: A simultaneous Probit-Tobit model. *Review of Economics and Statistics* 62: 77–83.

Congressional Quarterly. 1994. *Congressional Quarterly Guide to Congress.* Washington, DC: Congressional Quarterly Press.

Cook, Charlie. 2001. Whip's race is personal for House Democrats. *National Journal* (October 16): 3112–14.

Cooper, Joseph and David W. Brady. 1981. Institutional context and leadership style: The House from Cannon to Rayburn. *American Political Science Review* 75 (June): 411–25.

Cover, Albert D. 1977. One good term deserves another: The advantage of incumbency in congressional elections. *American Journal of Political Science* 21(3): 523–41.

Cox, Gary and Eric Magar. 1999. The value of majority status in the House. *American Political Science Review* 93(2):299–310.

Cox, Gary and Mathew McCubbins. 2005. *Setting the Agenda: Responsible Party Government in the U.S. House of Representatives.* Cambridge: Cambridge University Press.

———. 1997. Toward a theory of legislative rules changes: Assessing Shickler and Rich's evidence." *American Journal of Political Science* 41(4): 1376–86.

———. 1994. Bonding, structure, and the stability of political parties: Party government in the House. *Legislative Studies Quarterly* 4: 381–407.

———. 1993. *Legislative Leviathan: Party Government in the House.* Berkeley: University of California Press.

Crook, Sara Brandes and John R. Hibbing. 1985. Congressional reform and party discipline: The effects of changes in the seniority system on party loyalty in the U.S. House of Representatives. *British Journal of Political Science* 15: 207–26.

Currinder, Marian L. 2003. Leadership PAC contribution strategies and House member ambitions. *Legislative Studies Quarterly* 28:551–77.

———. 1998. Two-fisted giving: Big donors using leadership PACs for end-runs around contribution limits. *Capital Eye: A Close up Look at Money in Politics* 5(5) http://www.opensecrets.org/newsletter/ce55/index.htm.

Damore, David F. and Thomas Hansford. 1999. The allocation of party-controlled campaign resources in the House of Representatives, 1989–1996. *Political Research Quarterly* 52(June): 371–85.

Davidson, Russell and James G. MacKinnon. 1993. *Estimation and Inference in Econometrics.* New York: Oxford University Press.

Davidson, Roger and Walter Oleszek. 2004. *Congress and its Members.* 9th ed. Washington, DC: Congressional Quarlterly Press.

Deering, Christopher and Paul Wahlbeck. 2006. U.S. House Committee Chair Selection: Republicans Play Musical Chairs in the 107th Congress. *American Politics Research* 34(2): 223–42.

Den Hartog, Chris. 2005. The Jeffords Switch and Party Members' Success in the U.S. Senate. Paper presented at the 2005 meetings of the American Political Science Association, Chicago.

Dion, Douglas and John D. Huber. 1996. Procedural choice and the House Committee on Rules. *Journal of Politics* 58: 25–53.

Downs, Anthony. 1957. *An Economic Theory of Democracy.* New York: Harper.

Erickson, Robert and Gerald C. Wright. 1980. Policy Representation of Constituency Interests. *Political Behavior* 2: 91–106.

Evote. 2002. Rep. Kaptur Joins Democratic Leader Race. *Evote News* (November 14) http://www.evote.com/index.asp?Page=/news_section/2002-11/11142002kaptur.asp; accessed March 22, 2004.

Fenno, Richard. 1973. *Congressmen in Committees.* Boston: Little, Brown.

———. 1966. *The Power of the Purse: Appropriations Politics in Congress.* Boston: Little, Brown.

Ferejohn, John. 1977. On the decline of competition in congressional elections. *American Political Science Review* 71(1): 166–76.

Finnocchiaro, Charles and David Rohde. 2002. "War for the Floor: Agenda Control and the Relationship between Conditional Party Government and Cartel Theory." Paper presented at the 2002 meetings of the Midwest Political Science Association.

Foerstel, Karen. 2001. Pelosi's vote-counting prowess earns her the House Democrats' No. 2 spot. *Congressional Quarterly Weekly Report* (October 13): 2397–98.

Gelman, Andres and Hal Stern. 2005. The difference between "significant" and "not significant" is not itself statistically significant. Manuscript available on-line at http://www.stat.columbia.edu/~gelman/research/unpublished/signifrev.pdf.

Gierzynski, Anthony. 1992. *Legislative Party Campaign Committees in the American States.* Lexington: University of Kentucky Press.

Gilligan, Thomas and Keith Krehbiel. 1987. Collective decision-making and standing committees: An information rationale for restrictive amendment procedures. *Journal of Law Economics and Organization* 3(2): 287–335.

Glasgow, Garrett. 2002. The efficiency of Congressional campaign committee contributions in House elections. *Party Politics* 8(6): 657–72.

———. 1998. Strategic distribution of party resources. Political Methodology paper series on-line at http://web.polmeth.ufl.edu//papers/98/glasg 98b.pdf.

Goodliffe, Jay M. 2007. Campaign war chests and challenger quality in Senate elections. *Legislative Studies Quarterly* 32: 135–56.

———. 2004. War chests as precautionary savings. *Political Behavior* 26: 289–315.

———. 2001. The effect of war chests on challenger entry in U.S. House elections. *American Journal of Political Science* 45(4):833–44.

Gopoian, David. 1984. What makes PACs tick? An analysis of the allocation patterns of economic interest groups. *American Journal of Political Science* 28: 259–81.

Grenzke, Janet M. 1989. PACs and the Congressional supermarket: The currency is complex. *American Journal of Political Science* 33(1):1–24.

Grier, Kevin and Michael Munger. 1993. Corporate, labor, and trade association contributions to the U.S. House and Senate, 1978–1976. *Journal of Politics* 55: 614–43.

———. 1991. Committee assignments, constituent preferences, and campaign contributions to House incumbents. *Economic Inquiry* 29: 24–43.

Grove, Lloyd. 2002. Revving up their engines against SUVs. *Washington Post* (November 14): C3.

Hall, Richard L. and Frank W. Wayman 1990. Buying time: Moneyed interests and the mobilization of bias in Congressional committees. *American Political Science Review* 84(3): 797–820.

Heberlig, Eric S. 2003. Congressional parties, fundraising, and committee ambition. *Political Research Quarterly* 56: 151–61.

Heberlig, Eric S., Marc Hetherington, and Bruce A. Larson. 2006. The price of leadership: Campaign money and the polarization of congressional parties. *Journal of Politics* 68: 989–1002.

Heberlig, Eric S. and Bruce Larson. 2007. Party fundraising, descriptive representation, and the battle for majority control: Shifting leadership appointment strategies in the U.S. House of Representatives, 1990–2002. *Social Science Quarterly* 88:404–21.

———. 2005. Redistributing campaign funds by U.S. House members: The spiraling costs of the permanent campaign. *Legislative Studies Quarterly* 30:597–624.

Herrnson, Paul. 2004. *Congressional Elections: Campaigning at Home and in Washington.* Washington, DC: Congressional Quarterly Press.

———. 1986. Do parties make a difference? The role of party organizations in Congressional Elections. *Journal of Politics* 48: 589–615.

Hinckley, Barbara. 1971. *The Seniority System in Congress.* Bloomington: Indiana University Press.

Homans, George C. 1961. *Social Behavior.* New York: Harcourt, Brace & World.

———. 1958. Social behavior as exchange. *American Journal of Sociology,* 63: 597–606.

Jacobson, Gary C. 2004. *The Politics of Congressional Elections,* 6th ed. New York: Longman.

———. 1985–86. Party organization and distribution of campaign resources: Republicans and Democrats in 1982. *Political Science Quarterly* 100: 603–25.

———. 1980. *Money in Congressional Elections.* New Haven: Yale University Press.

Jenkins, Jeffery A. 1999. Examining the bonding effects of party: A comparative analysis of roll-call voting in the U.S. and Confederate Houses. *American Journal of Political Science* 43: 1144–65.

Jones, Mary Lynn F. 2002. Woman on top: Nancy Pelosi is the Democrats' mid-course correction. *American Prospect* (December 16): 11.

Kalt, Joseph P. and Mark A. Zupan. 1984. Capture and ideology in the economic theory of politics. *American Economic Review* 74: 279–300.

Kanthak, Kristin. 2007. Crystal elephants and committee chairs: Campaign contributions and leadership races in the U.S. House of Representatives. *American Politics Research* 35: 389–406.

Kaplan, Jonathan E. 2007. Obey: Late vote for Pelosi had nothing to do with term limits. *Hill* (January 16): 3.

Kingdon, John W. 1989. *Congressmen's Voting Decisions.* 3rd ed. Ann Arbor: University of Michigan Press.

Kolodny, Robin. 1998. *Pursuing Majorities: Congressional Campaign Committees in American Politics*. Norman: University of Oklahoma Press.

Krehbiel, Keith. 2000. Party discipline and measures of partisanship. *American Journal of Political Science* 44(2): 212–27.

———. 1993. Where's the party? *British Journal of Political Science* 23: 235–66.

———. 1991. *Information and Legislative Organization*. Ann Arbor: University of Michigan Press.

Kuhn, Jennifer. 1999. "The Movement of Money and Majorities." PhD diss.; University of California, San Diego.

Lee, Christopher. 2002. Still challenging Pelosi to lead House Democrats. *Washington Post* (November 11): A4.

Levendusky, Matthew S., Jeremy C. Pope, and Simon Jackman. 2005. Measuring District Level Preferences with Implications for the Analysis of U.S. Elections. Paper presented at the 2005 Political Methodology Society Conference, Tallahassee, Florida.

Lindell, Chuck. 2002. Election 2002: Two vie for Gephardt's post. *Atlanta Journal-Constitution* (November 8): 16A.

Magleby, David and Candice Nelson. 1990. *The Money Chase* Washington, DC: Brookings.

Martinez, Gebe. 2002. Solidly backed by her colleagues, Pelosi faces GOP's sharpened barbs. *Congressional Quarterly Weekly Report* (November 16): 3008–13.

Mayhew, David. 1974. *Congress: The Electoral Connection*. New Haven: Yale University Press.

McFadden, Daniel. 1974. Conditional logit analysis of qualitative choice behavior. In *Frontiers in Econometrics*, ed. P. Zarembka, 105–42. New York: Academic Press.

Miller, Warren E. and Donald E. Stokes. 1963. Constituency influence in Congress. *American Political Science Review* 57: 45–56.

Milyo, Jeffrey. 2001. What do candidates maximize (and why should anyone care)? *Public Choice* 109: 119–39.

Munson, Richard. 1993. *The Cardinals of Capitol Hill: The Men and Women Who Control Government Spending*. New York: Grove Press.

Nokken, Timothy. 2000. Dynamics of congressional loyalty: Party defection and roll-call behavior, 1947–1997. *Legislative Studies Quarterly* 25 (3): 417–44.

Nolan, Martin. 2001. Historic election brewing in House. *Boston Globe* (October 5): A23.

Olson, Mancur. 1965. *The Logic of Collective Action.* Cambridge: Harvard University Press.

Peabody, Robert L. 1976. *Leadership in Congress.* Boston: Little, Brown.

Pearson, Kathryn. 2005. "Party Discipline in the Contemporary Congress: Rewarding Loyalty in Theory and in Practice." Ph.D. diss., University of California, Berkeley.

Polsby, Nelson W., Miriam Gallaher, and William Rundquist. 1969. The growth of the seniority system in the U.S. House of Representatives. *American Political Science Review* 63(3): 787–807.

Republican Mainstreet Partnership. 2003. Reynolds looks to 2004 Congressional election picture. *Mainstreet Memo* (October): 4.

Renka, Russell D. and Daniel Ponder. 2005. Committee seniority violations in the U.S. House. Paper presented at the annual meeting of the American Political Science Association, Washington, DC.

Ripley, Randall B. 1969. *Majority Party Leadership in Congress.* Boston: Little, Brown.

Rohde, David W. 1991. *Parties and Leaders in the Postreform House.* Chicago: University of Chicago Press.

Sabato, Larry J. and Glenn R. Simpson. 1996. *Dirty Little Secrets: The Persistence of Corruption in American Politics.* New York: Times Books.

Sala, Brian R. 2003. Party loyalty and committee leadership in the House 1921–1940. In *Party, Process, and Political Change in Congress: New Perspectives on the History of Congress*, eds. David W. Brady and Mathew D. McCubbins. 166–94. Palo Alto, CA: Stanford University Press.

Salisbury, Robert H. 1969. An exchange theory of interest groups. *Midwest Journal of Political Science* 13: 1–32.

Sandalow, Marc. 2002a. Decision time for House Democrats. *San Francisco Chronicle* (November 8): A1.

———. 2002b. Savvy, cash clinched job for Pelosi. *San Francisco Chronicle* (November 17): A3.

———. 2001. Democrat whip vote is Oct. 10. *San Francisco Chronicle* (September 29): p. B2.

Schlesinger, Joseph A. 1966. *Ambition and Politics.* Chicago: Rand McNally.

Schatz, Joseph J. 2005. Lewis wins favor of GOP leaders—and coveted Appropriations chair. *Congressional Quarterly Weekly* (January 10): 71.

Schneider, Judy. 2002. *House Standing Committee Chairs: Rules Governing Selection Procedures.* Congressional Research Service Report for Congress, #RS21165.

———. 2004. *House Subcommittees: Assignment Process.* Congressional Research Service Report for Congress, #98–610.

Sinclair, Barbara. 1995. *Legislators, Leaders, and Lawmaking.* Baltimore: Johns Hopkins University Press.

———. 1983. *Majority Leadership in the U.S. House.* Baltimore: Johns Hopkins University Press.

Sorauf, Frank J. 1992. *Inside Campaign Finance: Myths and Realities.* New Haven: Yale University Press.

Spiegelhalter, David J., Nicola G. Best, Bradley P. Carlin, and Angelika van der Linde. 2002. Bayesian measures of model complexity and fit. *Journal of the Royal Statistical Society: Series B (Statistical Methodology)* 64: 583–639.

Stein, Robert M. and Kenneth N. Bickers. 1995. *Perpetuating the Pork Barrel: Policy Subsystems and American Democracy.* New York: Cambridge University Press.

Stewart, Charles and Jonathan Woon. 2007. Congressional Committee Assignments, 103–109th Congresses. http://web.mit.edu/17.251/www/data_page.html.

Stone, Peter H. 1996. Leaders' PACs mine gold in San Diego. *National Journal* (August 17): 1768.

Thomma, Steven. 2002. Center-left split snarls Democrats. *Pittsburgh Post-Gazette* (November 10): A16.

Waldman, Sidney R. 1972. *Foundations of Political Action: An Exchange Theory of Politics.* Boston: Little, Brown.

Wallison, Ethan. 2002. Gephardt to step aside. *Roll Call* (November 7).

Ware, Alan. 1996. *Political Parties and Party Systems.* Oxford: Oxford University Press.

Wawro, Gregory. 2001. A panel-probit analysis of campaign contributions. *American Journal of Political Science* 45: 563–79.

Weingast, Barry and William Marshall. 1988. The industrial organization of Congress. *Journal of Political Economy* 96: 132–63.

Weisman, Jonathan. 2007. Emerging grievances within party likely to test Pelosi. *Washington Post* (January 22): A05.

White, Joseph. 1989. "The Functions and Power of the House Appropriations Committee." Ph.D. diss., University of California, Berkeley.

Wilcox, Clyde. 1990. Member to member giving. In *Money, Elections, and Democracy,* eds. Margaret Latus Nugent and John R. Johannes. 168–86. Boulder: Westview Press.

———. 1989. Share the wealth: Contributions by congressional incumbents to the campaigns of other candidates. *American Politics Quarterly* 17(4): 386–408.

Wilcox, Clyde and Marc Genest. 1991. Member PACs as strategic actors. *Polity* 23(3): 461–70.

Willis, Derek. 2002. House GOP leadership places 'Cardinals' on precarious perch. *Congressional Quarterly Weekly Report* (November 16): 3015.

Wilson, Woodrow. 1885. *Congressional Government.* New York: Houghton Mifflin.

Wright, John. 1996. *Interest Groups and Congress: Lobbying, Contributions, and Influence.* Boston: Allyn and Bacon.

Wright, Gerald C. and Brian F. Schaffner. 2002. The influence of party: Evidence from state legislatures. *American Political Science Review* 96(2): 367–79.

Court Cases

Buckley v. Valeo, 424 U.S. 1 (1976).

Colorado Republican Federal Campaign Committee v. FEC, 518 U.S. 604 (1996).

Index

Abram, Michael E., 52
Aldrich, John H., xii, 4, 26, 28, 30, 38, 39, 40, 55, 57, 78
ambition, 29–30; electoral, 30, 32, 39; exchange theory and, 30, 34–35, 97; member contributions and, 25; power in Washington, 33–34, 57–58
Ansolabehere, Stephen, 25
Appropriations Committee (House), 4, 77; chair of, 71, 79–80; culture of, 78, 80, 81, 85–86; party influence on, 78–79; subcommittee chairs of, 77, 80–81, 97–98; subcommittee chair selection, 77, 80–81, 83–84; 86; 97–98. *See also* seniority; member contributions; party unity; ideological proximity
Armey, Richard, 21

Baker, Richard, 2
Baker, Ross, 1
Banking and Financial Services Committee (House), 2–3, 62
Battista, James S. Coleman, 39
Bedlington, Anne, 1, 26, 33
Bipartisan Campaign Reform Act of 2002 (BCRA), 5, 8, 9, 95, 101
Blunt, Roy, 22, 23, 95
Boehlert, Sherwood, 106
Boehner, John, 51–52, 95
Bonior, David, 92, 104
Boustany, Charles, Jr., 33

Box-Steffensmeier, Janet, 10
Brady, David W., 30, 37, 53
Brewer, Paul R., 65
Buchler, Justin, 9
Buckley v. Valeo, 7–8
bundling, 92
Burton, Phil, 90

Cannon, Joseph, 52; revolt against, 53, 98
Canon, David, 93
Cantor, David, 3, 28, 40
Cantor, Eric, 23
Capito, Shelly Moore, 33
Caro, Robert, 7
Carson, Jamie, xii, 41
Chappell, Henry W., 41
Colorado Republican Federal Campaign Committee v. FEC, 58
committee chair selection, 51, 97–98; 104th Congress, 65–66; 105th–106th Congresses, 66–67; 107th–109th Congresses, 67–68, 70–72; 110th Congress, 73; ideological proximity and, 52; member contributions and, 34, 60, 63, 67–72, 97–98; party unity and, 34, 63, 67–68, 70–72; post reform era, 54–55; Republican era rules for, 55–56; seniority and, 4, 52–53, 64, 65, 67, 70–72, 97–98
committee chairs: powers of, 53–54; significance of, 4; term limits on, 2, 55, 61, 75

Obey, David, 73, 107
Oleszek, Walter, 87
Olson, Mancur, 27
Oxley, Michael, 2, 22

partisan organization, 75
party cartel theory, 28, 30, 35, 49, 98;
 committee chair selection and, 57, 75;
 exchange theory and, 30–31, 39–40,
 48–49, 75, 98; institutional sources of
 party strength and, 38; promotion of
 party unity, 28, 49
party committees: contributions from, 28;
 contributions and party unity, 3, 40,
 43, 45–46, 47, 48
party fund-raising, as a collective
 action problem, 27. *See also* member
 contributions
party goals, 32, 81–82; majority control,
 32, 58; party unity, 39, 40, 48, 58
party independent expenditures, 43, 58
party leadership: advancement in, 22–23;
 fund-raising and, 32, 91–92, 94
 (*see also* member contributions)
party leadership selection, 4, 87–88,
 94–95; balancing, 93–94; fund-raising
 and, 91–92, 94, 95; ideology and,
 89–90, 91; member contributions and,
 91, 97–98; secret ballot, 90, 92
party strength, 28, 29, 37–40, 98,
 99–100; committee chairs and, 51
party unity, 48; Appropriations subcommittee chair selection and, 81, 84; committee assignments and, 80; committee
 chair selection and, 60–61, 63, 98;
 CQ scores, 42–43, 61; determinants of,
 42–44, 45, 48; exchange theory and, 48;
 leadership quality and, 100; member
 contributions to promote, 1–2, 3, 28,
 40, 43, 45, 46–47
party-coordinated expenditures, 43
Peabody, Robert L., 87, 93
Pearson, Kathryn, 41
Pelosi, Nancy: House minority leader
 campaign, 88–93, 94, 108; House

minority whip campaign, 91–92, 94;
 member contributions from, 21, 22,
 23; term limits and, 73
Petri, Thomas, 52
political action committee (PAC), 8, 26;
 contributions and roll-call voting,
 40–41. *See also* leadership PAC
Polsby, Nelson, 52, 59
Ponder, Daniel, 66
principal campaign committee (PCC), 8;
 contributions from and committee
 chair selection, 60; contributions from
 and party unity, 43. *See also* member
 contributions

Rangel, Charles, 21, 22
Reed, Thomas, 52
Regula, Ralph, 23, 80, 107
Reid, Harry M. 34
Renka, Russell, 66
Republican Steering Committee, 52, 55,
 61, 78
Reyes, Silvestre, 73
Reynolds, Thomas M., 23, 40
Ripley, Randall, 37
Rogers, Harold D., 23
Rohde, David, xii, 4, 26, 28, 30, 38, 39,
 54, 55, 57, 77, 78
Roukema, Marge, 2
Rundquist, William, 52, 59

Sabato, Larry, 26
Sala, Brian, 53
Salisbury, Robert, 31
Schlesinger, Joseph, 29
Schultz, Debbie Wasserman, 86
seed money, 33
Select Committee on Intelligence
 (House), 73
seniority: absolute vs. relative, 59;
 Appropriations subcommittee chair
 selection and, 78, 81–82, 83–84, 86;
 committee chair selection and, 4,
 52–53, 64, 65, 67, 70–72, 97–98;
 exchange theory and, 58–59; full

Made in the USA
Lexington, KY
24 September 2013